THE
WARNER
BOYS

THE
WARNER
BOYS

*Our Family's Story of
Autism and Hope*

ANA & CURT WARNER

with Dave Boling

Published by Little A, New York
www.apub.com

Amazon, the Amazon logo, and Little A are trademarks of Amazon.com, Inc., or its affiliates.

ISBN-13: 9781503900561 (hardcover)
ISBN-10: 1503900568 (hardcover)
ISBN-13: 9781503901469 (paperback)
ISBN-10: 1503901467 (paperback)

Cover design by Faceout Studio, Derek Thornton
Cover photo by Kristopher Blais

Printed in the United States of America

First Edition

We would like to dedicate this book to our brave children, Jonathan, Austin, Christian, and Isabella. Life is more meaningful because of you. We love you!

Beareth all things, believeth all things, hopeth all things, endureth all things.

—1 Corinthians 13:7

And now abideth faith, hope, charity, these three; but the greatest of these is charity.

—1 Corinthians 13:13

Table of Contents

AUTHORS' NOTE

This isn't a book about autism as much as it is about the love and strength that autism led us to discover within ourselves.

We don't elaborate on causes, or effectiveness of treatments, because we're not scientists, we're not medical experts—we're parents. Our twins, Austin and Christian, have been profoundly affected by autism spectrum disorder (ASD) for more than twenty years. As one of the twins' doctors, John A. Green III, said, "Austin and Christian's story is so poignant, full of both despair and hope." That's what we've decided to share, the story of our family's journey through despair toward hope.

So many of our memories are still raw, and the retelling painful, but these stories are true. We want you to be able to see this through our eyes, and feel what's in our hearts.

After our sons began showing symptoms, many of our old friends and football fans thought we disappeared. The truth is, we were just focused on keeping our kids safe and getting them as healthy as possible. It was an isolation, but it was unintentional.

A few other things about our story:

We don't pretend to have the answers for everybody. Our story doesn't suggest a right way or a wrong way of caring for children with ASD. We're not authorities or superparents. We've made a ton of mistakes. If there are heroes in this story, they're our kids.

Everyone copes and heals in different ways. We have faith in Christ Jesus, our Lord and Savior, but don't want to come off as preachy. We mention our beliefs when recounting our darkest times and when we relied most heavily on that faith. We'd be unreliable narrators if we ignored it.

We don't want to get into the popular debates surrounding the cause of autism. Up front: we believe kids should be vaccinated, but we worry about the volume and frequency of the vaccinations, and the health of the children when they get them. We came away with these concerns because of our experiences with Austin and Christian. To each his own. We don't want to argue; we want as much energy and effort as possible directed at finding ways to stem the rising incidence of this disorder.

We hope you will see that ours is a love story. It's a love that's been tested by fire and by death and by heartache and by so many of the other divisive factors that try to tear families apart. By the grace of God, we made it through together. This is a story about the love of a family, and how we managed to make it last.

—Ana and Curt Warner

THE
WARNER
BOYS

Austin and Christian, age three.

CHAPTER 1

THE DIAGNOSIS

July 1994–June 1999

ANA

Our son Austin devoured books. Not reading them, eating them. His twin brother, Christian, also ate strange things, like string and fabric. We had no idea why they were doing it, and when we asked questions of other parents and pediatricians, nobody else seemed to understand it, either. Don't be too alarmed, we were told often when the twins were between two and five, all children are different and can be puzzling with the phases they go through.

None of our early concerns diminished the joy we felt at having three healthy and happy sons. The twins were a bit of a surprise, coming along eighteen months after our first son, Jonathan. In my mind, we were on track and blessed in so many ways. I always had been one to dream about the "perfect life" I wanted to live. Even when I was a little girl, I tried to envision how my life would be. This was it. In fact, this was even better than I could have imagined. I was delighted to be a stay-at-home mom while Curt continued developing his car dealership in suburban Seattle after having retired from his eight-season NFL career. I was so proud of him; he had such success as a running back with the Seahawks, and now he was applying the same kind of dedication and hard work to his car business.

When the twins reached two, their personalities started changing. They always loved hugging and being held, and wrestling around with Jonathan, but at that point they started pulling away from physical contact. It was as if the activities they loved had started irritating them. At first, I rationalized it as them beginning to find their unique personalities. We'd never had twins, so maybe their gaining distance from us was common for children in multiple births. Their behavior worsened as they grew, though, to the point where I was certain this was more than just one of those cranky stages that kids go through. Persistent gnawing on chairs and tables and windowsills was nothing we'd seen from Jonathan.

I'd never seen kids with such energy. They almost never slept. So naturally, we didn't, either. We couldn't take our eyes off them, especially Austin, who could be so quick. Sometimes he'd reach down to pick up something off the sidewalk, such as a worm, and if we didn't get to him fast enough, he'd eat it. Austin climbed everywhere. He was fearless, like a tiny daredevil lacking any sense of caution or concern for self-endangerment. He had no innate fear of getting hurt. He also had a particular knack for finding ways to get things he wanted even if we had hidden them for his own protection, and for figuring out how to sneak away and get into mischief.

These behaviors were unnerving for us as parents, but one thing beyond those concerns really alarmed us: the twins were both growing increasingly angry and aggressive. They were hostile with each other, with Jonathan, and with us. Hitting, slapping, biting. Ever more frequently, this simmering anger would erupt into inconsolable rage. Life became a succession of crying fits, which were so frantic and so all-consuming that we started calling them "meltdowns." I believe that parents, especially mothers, have great insights into who their children really are, deep down, and can truly identify what makes them tick. But we were at such a loss to understand Austin and Christian, and so many unexpected behaviors were coming at us that it became hard to sort through it all. Even when they were calm, the twins no longer interacted and communicated normally, sometimes sitting alone, sullen.

Almost every night after we would put the kids to bed, Curt and I would huddle in our room for a few quiet moments to compare thoughts, to sort through the events of the day, to try to make sense of it all. It was like we were debriefing each other, as if we needed the other's thoughts to verify what we were seeing and feeling. Curt assured me that all of this chaos wasn't just in my head, that I wasn't imagining what was happening. Our discussion would end, and, exhausted from the day, we'd give each other a kiss and try to drop off to sleep, only to be awakened within minutes by one of the twins banging on something. We were in a cycle of anxiety-fueled days and sleepless nights.

For almost three years, we worked our way through the lengthy list of pediatricians, giving one doctor after another the full account of the twins' behaviors. One doctor handed Austin a tongue depressor to occupy his interest while he asked me a few questions. By the time the doctor charted his notes and looked back at Austin, he had chewed the stick down to nothing. Austin *ate* the tongue depressor. Chewed it up completely. He'd done it almost as if on cue to illustrate my claims.

"See, that's what I'm talking about," I told the doctor. He was stunned. Said he had never seen anything like it. But like all of the twins' exams from roughly age two through almost five, the doctor's assessment resulted in no definitive diagnosis.

As time went on, the twins' language skills failed to develop, and instead of gaining new words, they began constructing a confusing vocabulary of their own. Early on, doctors told us this sometimes was a pattern common to twins, or might be the result of my speaking both English and Portuguese, my native language growing up in Brazil. I thought it might be good for the boys to grow up bilingual, as it's so much easier to learn languages at an early age. But I stopped the Portuguese immediately after talking to the doctor who thought it might be contributing to the twins' lack of verbal development. That might have been the first time that I worried that I was causing them to be behind schedule in their benchmarks. That was it—I was at fault.

Nothing we tried to correct the decline in their speaking and reasoning skills helped, though, and soon Austin and Christian were well below the charts in almost every developmental metric—language, socialization, cognitive awareness. Children are expected to be making sentences by age three, to play cooperatively by four, to know two thousand words by five. Curt would always examine the charts in the pediatricians' offices and notice that the twins were nowhere near the expected benchmarks. This deficit was especially true for Christian. The doctors said that developmental problems in twins can be particularly significant for a less-dominant twin like Christian. Male children tended to be slower with language, anyway, they assured us. We weren't reassured, though; our older son, Jonathan, hadn't had any language trouble or any of these other curious behaviors. Meanwhile, their tantrums grew more and more spectacular.

Even a quick trip to the store could lead to an emotional detonation. I remember going to Lowe's one time to get some supplies for yardwork. I wanted to be brave enough to take the three boys to the store and put them in the cart and go into the gardening area. There was a fairly strong smell of fertilizer when we walked in, and I can only guess that this is what set the twins off. They started screaming so loudly I had to turn around and get out of there. For the rest of that day—and many days after that—I felt like the worst mother in the world. How was it that I couldn't even take my boys shopping without creating such a scene? I couldn't help but notice how other shoppers looked at us—how they looked at me!

It wasn't surprising that people in the store would be curious. Before the twins, I had never seen children act like this, either. But their looks were so judgmental. What was I doing to these kids that upset them so? I must be mistreating these kids to get them screaming so loudly!

Jonathan, in the same circumstances and environment, continued to be so calm and easygoing. Only on rare occasions would the twins' behavior upset him. I could understand his anxiety when he would get caught in the middle of some of these meltdowns. The outbursts were frightening to Curt and me, so it had to be terrifying for a little boy. As our stress compounded with every sleepless night and troublesome day, Curt and I continued to second-guess ourselves. When doctors couldn't come up with anything, we were left to assume it was us, we were doing something wrong. It had to be some flaw in our nurturing. Didn't it? It had been one thing to think that I had inadvertently created the problems with their language skills, but it was far more hurtful to think that somehow I was causing my twins to be so unhappy and angry. As deeply as I looked, I couldn't find answers, and I beat myself up over it—especially as my young sons became more volatile.

As the twins' size and mobility increased, so did our challenges. Curt and I began to sleep in shifts so one of us could be on watch 24-7. We didn't have a choice. They'd get up in the middle of the night and be all over the house, getting into things, even climbing on furniture and then falling off. Those can be dangerous situations, so we had to beef up our defenses. We changed their bedroom doorknobs to put the lock on the outside so we could keep them in their room at night. We would set up a baby monitor so we could always be listening. At one point we tied their little toddler beds together; for a short while their being close to one another at night helped them sleep a little better. That didn't last, though.

During the day, the meltdowns grew more frequent, and nothing could be done to console them. When we tried to comfort them, they'd either strike out or withdraw further. Christian was particularly short fused. And when he wasn't upset, he was almost completely disconnected, lying in a corner, precisely lining up his toys, focused on it as if it were the most important thing in the world. We tried to get smarter, to become behavioral detectives, looking for clues and patterns in what would trigger a meltdown or cause them to disconnect. I started keeping track of everything we had done during the day and everything they had eaten. But there never was a common stimulus we could pinpoint.

Still, as confused and concerned as we were, no emotion was greater than our gratitude for the gift of these boys. It was difficult to be thankful specifically when we were in the heat of a meltdown, but all the while we knew what a blessing they were. Having already lost one child, we learned that nothing could be taken for granted. It wasn't ever the pressure or exhaustion that was most troubling to us; it was the realization that our boys were in a kind of pain we couldn't understand. For some unknown reason, everything was so hard for them. We felt we had to keep pushing doctors to find a way to help them.

In the early summer of 1999, as the twins were nearing five years old, we moved to Camas, in southwestern Washington, a growing suburb of Portland, Oregon. Curt had taken over a car dealership there; it seemed to be a better business opportunity, and the boys were still young enough that the move wouldn't be disrupting. The general manager at the new dealership took special interest when Curt happened to mention some of the twins' behaviors. He had a friend whose child had some behavioral issues and had been helped by seeing a doctor at Providence Portland Medical Center. He referred Curt to this doctor.

On June 10, 1999, exactly one month after we moved to Camas, we took Austin to see this doctor. The morning was overcast and gloomy. The doctor had told us that she wanted to see the twins one at a time, so we arranged to have a sitter come watch Jonathan and Christian. Taking Austin first made sense to us. He was the more advanced of the twins. He had slightly better language and social skills than Christian. His vocabulary was better, even though it consisted of just five words, all curiously related to Disney movies. We'd been stunned when we heard him say "Pocahontas" at a time when he couldn't say "mama."

The doctor was pleasant and professional—a specialist in developmental pediatrics. She talked to us about the boys' behavior for a few minutes as she watched Austin playing with toy cars on the floor nearby. She called to him, trying to get his attention, and tried to get him to look her in the face. Austin didn't respond. He was that way with us, too, when he was focused on something. Sometimes it would be as if he had withdrawn behind a curtain.

But that's how little boys are, right? They're busy. All little boys are like that, aren't they? I expected the doctor at some point to start a thorough exam, to check him over completely. Take some tests, perhaps. But she needed none of that. She had seen all she needed to see and had heard all she needed to hear from us. She leaned toward us and announced, "Your boy has autism." Her diagnosis seemed so abrupt, especially after so many doctors had made so many examinations over the years without coming up with a diagnosis.

At that time, awareness of autism was limited. I was certainly an example of that. The only frame of reference I had for autism was the movie *Rain Man*, with Dustin Hoffman. I thought back to the scenes of him flapping his hands, screaming and avoiding everyone's touch, and then suddenly getting so loud and hostile. It was a frightening image. I remembered the character having great math skills. Our boys hadn't shown any signs of those kinds of specific skills. Then I remembered that Hoffman's character spent his life hidden away from his family in an institution. I panicked at the thought. Would they try to do that with our twins? Would they take away our boys? I was lost in the horrible image of people coming to get our kids. Curt's mind must have been spinning, too, because neither one of us said a word in response. The doctor surely picked up on our confusion. "Your boy has autism," she said again.

I looked at Curt. His face was blank, his eyes were wide. We both looked down at Austin, playing quietly on the floor. He couldn't have this thing . . . this *autism*. After all the examinations both of the twins had, there was no way this doctor could see Austin for a mere few minutes and be so certain of the diagnosis. She'd done nothing more than watch him play. I was really proud of him; he'd been very good and well behaved and quiet. He hadn't thrown a tantrum or had a dramatic meltdown. How could she be so sure just from watching him play, and from our brief descriptions of his behaviors?

Yes, he was slow to speak and had some unusual habits. We thought maybe it was ADHD, we'd heard about that, it was all over the news. And there were pills for that, right? That wouldn't be the worst thing. But autism? Like Dustin Hoffman in that movie? We still hadn't responded.

"I'm sorry," the doctor stressed again. "Your son . . . has . . . autism."

"What did I do wrong?" It was the first question I asked the doctor.

"No, no, it's not your fault," the doctor said.

"How could it *not* be my fault? I'm their mother," I said. I'm sure it sounded like I was pleading for her to tell me it was my fault. I wanted to defend Austin, to take the blame for whatever was wrong. I started making excuses for him, listing anything I could think of that I might have done to cause the twins' behaviors.

I told her that I had gone through such deep emotional lows, after earlier pregnancies, that I had postpartum depression; maybe I'd been so torn apart by those experiences that I hadn't given the twins enough attention. I could do better. I promised I would. I was to blame, not the boys. I could be a better mother.

"No, it's not your fault," the doctor said again. She was very compassionate when she heard me trying to assume blame. "There was nothing you could have done. And there's really not much you can do now. There is no cure."

The room went silent, except for Austin's playing, as Curt and I took in those words: *no cure*. I thought, *Oh, no, if Austin has autism, and he's our healthier son, what will this mean for Christian?*

I don't remember a thing the doctor said after that. I wanted to leave before she told us something else hurtful and unfixable. I can't remember any instructions about what we should do next. Were there more specialists to see? What would lie ahead for the boys? What would lie ahead for us? I'm sure she must have told us some of these things, but I was in shock, and confused and afraid. I was numb, in fact. That was what it felt like: I'd gone completely numb.

Then came denial. Curt and I had been given so many theories by so many doctors for so many years. Why should we believe that this doctor got it right? We should schedule an appointment with another specialist as soon as possible. We should keep trying until somebody got it right. We couldn't stop until we got a diagnosis of something we could cure.

The drive home was thirty minutes. Or maybe it was three days. I don't remember anything about it. I was dazed, and still absolutely certain that this was all my fault. Curt was silent next to me in the car. Maybe he was also haunted by the idea that somebody might try to take our twin boys from us, to institutionalize them like the autistic Rain Man. Curt would never stand for that. It would get very ugly if somebody tried to take Curt's children from him. But Curt had gone so quiet, in such deep thought, that it frightened me.

When we got home, I raced to the computer and typed out a search for the word *autism*. I started seeing lists of behaviors that matched so much of what we'd experienced with the twins. I knew immediately the doctor was right. Autism was obviously the right diagnosis. There was no question. I was suddenly amazed—and upset. How was this the first time we'd heard the word mentioned? I no longer wondered how she had spotted it so fast, but rather why so many others had failed to spot it at all.

I kept going from one website to the next, taking notes, starting what would become a decades-spanning study of the disorder. From that moment, I knew we were going to be in for a long battle, but it was a relief in two important ways: first, at least we finally had a name for it, and second, maybe it wasn't my fault after all.

CHAPTER 2

COAL COUNTRY TO THE NFL

CURT

Our extended family occupied the last three houses at the far end of the tiny coal-mining town of Wyoming, West Virginia. The houses were tucked close to the banks of the Guyandotte River, one of the most polluted rivers in the state of West Virginia, filled with heavy metals and mine wastes. We didn't know any better and swam in it all the time. Whenever a hard rain came, my parents would get nervous about flooding. So we kids were haunted by the image of the river rising up and washing us away. It rose so near the house a few times that we had to move to higher ground and wait it out at the company store.

Our house was next to Preacher Warner's house. His given name was George, but everybody knew him as "Preacher." A hard-core evangelical Christian who was all about fire and brimstone, Preacher worked in the coal mines full-time but was a minister on the side. He was a character, always wearing a dark suit, white shirt, and tie—very clean and proper, with a little trimmed mustache. Preacher had a gospel radio show on Saturdays, and on Sunday mornings he'd give sermons at his little church in the unincorporated town. On Sunday afternoons, he and his wife, Lillie, would drive all over the county preaching at churches that didn't have their own ministers. Through the 1950s, '60s, and '70s, in the back hills of West Virginia, Preacher Warner taught the Gospel to an all-white congregation. The only black person in that church was the minister, and people came from all over to hear his sermons. On every other night of the week, he'd have Bible studies and gatherings at his house, right next to ours. We'd hear them over there singing and praying—like a spirited revival meeting at his house every night. It was something to see how his ministry unified the community.

Preacher had thirteen children, including my father, James, so I had a gazillion cousins around. I was among the youngest of my generation of Warners, so that meant I took the usual beatdowns from the older kids when we all got together.

When I call James and Lottie Mae Warner my parents, it's accurate in a legal and emotional sense. But biologically, they were my grandparents, and Preacher was my great-grandfather. My biological mother was James and Lottie Mae's daughter, but I was adopted by my grandparents at birth. I wouldn't say my relationship with my biological mother was estranged, it's just that she wasn't around. I never knew my biological father. My grandparents raised me, loved me, disciplined me, and taught me right from wrong. When I think of "Mom and Dad," it's them.

My father worked the night shift in the coal mines for forty years. In the evenings, some other miners would swing by and pick him up, and they'd drive to Coal Mountain, West Virginia, where he worked through the night. In the mornings, he'd come home with that black coal dust all over him. The mines were dangerous, of course, and we always heard stories about terrible accidents, but our family was fortunate. Dad never got trapped in a mine collapse or broke any bones or had any respiratory problems. He used to chew tobacco, which he claimed filtered out the coal dust. That might have just been his excuse to chew that stuff.

It wasn't only the hard work in the mines that made James Warner a man I admired. His unselfishness has been an inspiration to me all my life. Every morning when he came home, he'd give the kids some sweet treat that he had saved out of his lunch bucket. Here was a man working all those long hours—back-breaking labor—who would save some of his food because he knew it would be special for us. Looking back, what made it even more special was knowing it was a gift from his heart.

James Warner was my image of what a real man is.

My dad would sleep until midday, and in the summertime he'd spend the afternoons coaching our Little League team. He never missed a practice or a game even though that was time he could have been resting before going back to work. For as long as I could remember, I was always on a baseball diamond or some other kind of field, and he was there coaching me and my brother, Robert, and every other kid who was interested. He was an athletic and strong man, and his brothers also were known for being great athletes.

He was a surrogate dad to so many kids, teaching all of us to love sports. Not just the fundamentals of the games, but having respect for the games, and to play with sportsmanship and humility. Those lessons stayed with me even when I got to the NFL, and at times it was like he was still there on the field with me, whispering in my ear.

He knew being out there on the ball field was about more than teaching and coaching; it was about keeping kids on the straight and narrow. His mentorship of kids was a big part of why he was so well respected in the community. The only thing he asked in return was that we always worked to be our best. In sports. In school. In anything we did.

I'm sure we were like a lot of other families in those days; we struggled month to month to get by, and that meant food stamps and piling up credit at the company store. Until I was in the sixth or seventh grade, we didn't have an indoor bathroom, just the old outhouse. But to me, it felt like we were rich. My mother spoiled us. She did everything: cooked, cleaned, washed our clothes. She could really cook. I didn't realize what a great cook she was until I went off to college. She made cornbread and beans taste like a delicacy.

My mother also was the disciplinarian. She probably wasn't taller than five feet, but she was imposing. I could talk back a little bit to my father, but I would never dare with my mother. She'd get a paddle or a switch, and she knew how to use them. She kept us in line. My brother and I knew very well where her boundaries were, and she'd use whatever means necessary to make sure we didn't cross them.

We played a lot of sandlot sports when we were young. Robert was a year and a half older than I was. When you always play against somebody who's older, you have to figure out ways to beat him; you have to be creative and work harder. That was my goal in life when I was young—to beat my big brother. He was probably one of the best athletes I've ever been around. He could play anything and make it look easy, while I had to work harder to be good at it.

All my hard work started paying off when I reached my sophomore year at Pineville High. I was named to the all-state team in basketball that year, and the next year, I led the state in scoring in football. At first, I didn't have any aspirations beyond high school sports. As I got older, I started to sense that the only options for the future were to work in the coal mines or find a way to get out of the valley. I knew I didn't want to end up working as a coal miner. I'd watched how hard my father worked, and how tough the work was on him. So sports, and maybe getting a scholarship, started to seem like the best way to get out of that valley.

Getting a scholarship was pretty rare in the little coal towns of West Virginia, especially at Pineville, where my senior class had just ninety students. Still, some of the honors I'd received caused colleges to start sending me recruiting questionnaires. The college recruiters send these to prospective student-athletes before sending any coaches to visit. The thing was, I didn't really like the idea of filling out the questionnaires. It felt to me like they were asking me to brag about myself. Being humble was a major part of my father's lessons, so talking about how good you were wasn't something that was allowed in my family. It didn't seem like good sportsmanship, and it didn't seem to me like part of being a good person, either.

I was struggling with how to approach these forms, so my English teacher, Mrs. Libby McKinney, took over as my first informal public relations agent. I was a good student because my parents expected it of me. Mrs. McKinney appreciated that, but also saw something more in me than just being an athlete with good grades, so she wrote a letter about me to coach Joe Paterno at Penn State. She was convinced I could be a good student-athlete for them, and she told him so, clipping some of the articles out of the local sports pages and sending them along with the letter. Mrs. McKinney was an example of how a caring teacher, willing to go the extra mile, can have a profound impact on a student's life. I might be working in the coal mines today without her stepping in and getting involved.

Word started getting around to other schools about me, and coaches from around the country got busy scouting me really quickly—even without letters from Mrs. McKinney. By the time my senior football season was over, coaches were visiting Pineville to meet me and watch me play in basketball games to get an idea of what kind of athlete I was. Coach Jackie Sherrill came down from Pittsburgh. Tom Osborne came all the way from Nebraska. Pitt had recently won a national championship, and Nebraska was always a powerhouse, so it was flattering they'd come down to West Virginia hill country just to see me. As I recall, Sherrill and Paterno came down on the same night to watch me play in a basketball game. They must have wanted to see me pretty badly, because they flew down in small planes on a very snowy night.

My parents and I really liked Coach Paterno. It was important for me to go someplace close enough that my parents could drive to games. I knew it was important for them, too, although they didn't put any pressure on me. I wanted them to share in whatever success I might attain; I wanted it to feel like it was a reward for everything they'd done for me. Penn State wasn't quite four hundred miles from Pineville, and they would be able to drive up to State College, Pennsylvania, on game weekends. It wasn't right next door by any means, but we all agreed Penn State was the right fit.

Even before classes started, we were thrown into football training camp, which included three practices a day in the blazing heat. It was a tough camp, physically, and it was also the first time I was away from home. During those first weeks, I was homesick, probably like a lot of kids are. Being from such a small town, and being used to the small-school level of competition, made this seem like an enormous step for me. But always at the front of my mind was how many people were pulling for me. I didn't want to let anybody down by quitting and heading back to West Virginia.

I remember early in training camp going into the office of running backs coach Fran Ganter to check out the depth chart. I was just a freshman from a little town, so my name was the last on the list, with some great players ahead of me. I was eighteen years old and only weighed about 180 pounds. I'd be lucky, I thought, if I saw any action at all as a freshman.

When my parents and the McKinneys came up to Penn State for my first game, against Rutgers, I reminded them that this wasn't Pineville High anymore. Beaver Stadium held seventy-seven thousand back then, which was roughly seventy-five times bigger than the entire population of Pineville. They gave me the chance to return the opening kickoff, and I broke free from the coverage and almost ran for a touchdown. My family said later that fans around them in the stands were looking at their programs, trying to find out who this new kid was wearing number 25. That kickoff return also got the coaches' attention, and after we had the ball the first few times, Coach Ganter came over to the bench and told me I was going in at running back the next time the offense was on the field.

I looked at him like, *Uh, me?* I thought I'd had a pretty good training camp, but that was just practice. There were so many more-experienced players on the team at the running back position. I looked around the stadium. It was packed. More people than I'd ever seen in one place in my life, and I remembered the things my father taught me about competing and focusing on doing my best. When I did that, the crowd disappeared. I was just out there playing football, and I was confident about what I could do on the field.

In one of my early carries, I ran for a touchdown. I had run for a lot of touchdowns in high school, but this, coming in my first college game, in front of so many people, was such a special feeling. I ended the game with three touchdowns and one hundred rushing yards. Coach Paterno was never one to pump up a player too much, especially a freshman, but I could tell he was very happy with how I played. I had felt strongly that I could make it at Penn State, but I didn't have any clue it would happen that quickly.

From the first days at Penn State, I had such a deep respect for Coach Paterno, for his values and what he meant to the Penn State tradition. He ran a tight ship, and the rules were for everybody—stars included. It wasn't just lip service. I saw him bench All-American players if they didn't follow the rules. That meant succeeding in the classroom, too, and behaving well off the field. I always felt Coach Paterno was a man of high integrity who lived up to his word. Our team took on Joe's personality, and there was a bond of mutual respect among the players and coaches. It was the type of camaraderie and common purpose that I don't think you can find in many places in life. It was such a great and proud tradition that we had at Penn State, so it was very painful and disappointing when it was tarnished by scandal near the end of Coach Paterno's career. I could never imagine such things happening there, and I can say I never saw or heard of any problems related to inappropriate or criminal behavior by staff members in the program during my years there.

I'm proud that while I was a player at Penn State, we won our first national football championship (1982) and twice I was named All-American (1981–82). My mom was proudest of my degree in speech communications. Her pride was especially significant to me because she was having such a tough time with her health, which my family had tried to keep concealed from me while I was at school. She didn't want me to find out because she knew I'd worry, and maybe I'd decide to come home, or I'd lose focus on school. While I was away, her blood pressure and diabetes had gotten much worse. I understood why they kept it from me, but I later felt I had missed that time with her. And the uncertainty surrounding her health was something that drove me after my final season at Penn State. I wanted to get ready for the draft so Mom could see me in the NFL.

In 1983, Chuck Knox was the new coach of the Seattle Seahawks, having already had years of success coaching the Los Angeles Rams and Buffalo Bills. Knox relied on the rushing attack so heavily that his offense was nicknamed "Ground Chuck," so the first thing he went looking for when he took over the Seahawks was a running back. Knox and his wife, Shirley, came to visit me at Penn State. We had lunch together, and he asked me if I had any problems coming all the way out to Seattle. It was something I had to think about. The West Coast was a long way for my family to travel to see me play. It was a serious concern for me, especially once I learned of my mother's health issues.

Chuck reminded me that the Seahawks often played road games in the East and Midwest—close enough for my family to attend—and that was something that made a move to Seattle easier to consider.

I knew that if Knox loved giving the ball to running backs, he'd surely develop a good offensive line to do the blocking. That appealed to me a great deal. He was also known as a tough guy from western Pennsylvania. Growing up in a coal-mining area, and then playing at Penn State, I knew a lot of guys like Chuck—hard-nosed, no nonsense. I knew I'd be comfortable playing for him. When we met, he said a lot of things I wanted to hear about the kind of football he wanted to play. His coaching would be good for my career. Yes, sir, I told him, Seattle would work just fine for me.

I flew out to California for draft day to be at the house of my agent, Marvin Demoff, who also represented high-profile players like John Elway and Dan Marino. He was involved in a lot of draft-day drama with those quarterbacks. But in the meantime, he also was working a deal with the Seahawks, who traded up from the number 9 pick to get me in the number 3 spot in the draft.

There were six future Hall of Fame players taken in the first round of that draft. Elway went first. Eric Dickerson second. Then me.

The transaction cost the Seahawks their first-, second-, and third-round picks that year. For a team that had a lot of needs across the roster, that was a huge investment in me. It made it clear they really wanted me, and that was very meaningful. It also meant that Chuck Knox was going to expect me to immediately jump in and help improve the offense. It felt like an exciting start of a new chapter in my life, and I couldn't help but think about how far I'd come from Pineville High. With that in mind, there were some things I felt I needed to do before I left West Virginia for Seattle.

The first thing I did when I got some of my NFL money was to move my dad and mom up off that riverbank in Wyoming and into a house in Pineville. My dad was prideful and a little stubborn about me doing anything for them, but he knew the house would make my mom happy. After arguing with me about it for a while, he finally went along with it. Second, I went down to that company store and paid off our family debts.

After my parents were settled in their new house on higher ground, the Guyandotte River rose up in a great flood one day and washed our old house away.

Seahawks fans were ripe for a winning season when I got there. They'd never had a playoff team, but their fans still had that expansion-club fervor. Even when they were losing, they made the Kingdome hell for opposing teams, giving us a nice home field advantage, but loud fans aren't enough if you don't have the talent.

Chuck Knox had a simple scheme. It certainly wasn't a situation where I had to come in and learn a complex offense. He told me, "Run to daylight" and "Run where they ain't." That was it. To me, the beauty of a run-to-daylight offense was that nobody told me where I had to go—I could use my instincts, and that suited my style. I could read the blocking and how the holes were developing, and once I got there, decide whether to go right or left. Chuck asked every lineman to get his helmet on a man and shield him the best he could. It was up to me to find the cracks and slip through. Somewhere amid all those collisions, I was supposed to find open grass. Chuck didn't like his ballcarriers to do a lot of dancing around in the backfield. I was allowed to make one cut and head upfield for as many yards as I could get.

My rookie season ended up being better than I could have expected. We went 9–7 and made the playoffs with a wild card berth—the first postseason appearance in franchise history. Suddenly, the Seahawks owned Seattle. It had always been a college-football town, with the University of Washington being the popular team, but it felt like the

Seahawks had become king that season. Once we made the playoffs, we really made some noise, beating the Denver Broncos 31–7 in the first round. That meant we had to go on the road to Miami the next week, meeting a Dolphins team that had been in the Super Bowl the previous season and had won their division with a 12–4 record. Of course, we were heavy underdogs, but that was just how Chuck liked it. We won the game 27–20 by playing Chuck's favorite way—running the football. I carried the ball twenty-nine times for 113 yards and two touchdowns that day.

The next game would be the AFC Championship game against the Raiders—one game away from the Super Bowl. The Seahawks were no longer a quirky expansion team at a remote NFL outpost. We were on the map. We lost to the Raiders, but expectations were established for the next season. I had finished my rookie year leading the conference in rushing with more than 1,400 yards, was named AFC Offensive Player of the Year, and earned my first Pro Bowl honor.

It's hard to describe what running the football in the NFL feels like. I tell people it's controlled chaos—thrilling and terrifying at the same time. There's uncertainty and there are consequences, and the one constant is knowing there's always going to be contact. A lot of contact. Often very violent contact. You get hit from every angle every time you carry the ball, often by multiple guys going as hard and as fast as they can. You have the ball in your hands, and all eleven of your opponents want to hit you. Inevitably, that involves pain.

There were some obvious differences between playing NFL and college football—the NFL was a business, and it felt like a job. The veterans didn't really care much for rookies, and the new guys experienced some hazing. I was in charge of bringing doughnuts to the headquarters for the vets, for instance. Chuck's teams were always loaded with veteran leaders, and a lot of times they were pretty old-school about how things worked. I didn't play like a rookie, though, and I could tell I had earned their respect after that first season. There's nothing a young player can do to fit in that is more important than helping the veterans win football games.

A lot of experts were picking us as a title contender in 1984, and I was certain I could improve on my rookie season. I would need that kind of production if we were to reach the expectations for us as a team.

As loud as it got in the Kingdome, it was not a great stadium for football. The Seattle Mariners had started playing in the Kingdome before we did, and the field was a hard artificial surface, Astroturf, which was better suited to baseball than football. When we played on it, we used to wear soccer cleats, which were thought to give us the best traction. As we started the second quarter of the 1984 season opener against Cleveland, I took a pitch to the right and, just as I had hundreds of times before, planted my foot to cut inside against the pursuit. My cleats bit hard, and I went one way and my leg went the other. I knew it was bad before I even hit the turf. An athlete knows when something has gone wrong with their body. And this felt *very* wrong. It was confirmed by the way the doctors looked at me and by how silent the stadium went. As soon as I got off the field, team doctor Pierce Scranton told me we had to get to the hospital immediately so he could operate. I tore my anterior cruciate ligament (ACL), and in those days it was considered a probable career-ending injury. Running backs just didn't come back from ACL rebuilds. Or if they did, they were never the same.

It was a tough time for me, but the love I received from the Seahawks fans made me feel good, and I was very appreciative. The local phone company sent over a get-well message that was 1,449 yards long—the same distance I gained rushing my rookie season. The fans loved their Seahawks, and that made it an exciting place to be. The Seahawks rallied to the best season in franchise history that year, winning twelve of sixteen games. I was thrilled for our success, but every player wants to be a part of it, so while I was happy for them, I was miserable about not being able to contribute on the field. It sounds selfish to admit it, but that part of it was bittersweet. I wanted to be on the field. That feeling pushed me even harder to get back to the level of play I was at before the injury.

During the rehabilitation, I was working out for six to eight hours a day at the team facility, and it wasn't fun. It was painful and exhausting and tedious, and it seemed like there was no end in sight. Certainly there were no guarantees. Trainers Jimmy Whitesel and John Kasik did a great job of pushing me through the rehab process, despite the fact that every couple of months I'd get mad at them and just go home for a couple of days. Maybe I was dealing with some uncertainty about whether I'd ever get back to what I'd been. I had reason to be confident in my abilities, in what I could do on the field when I was healthy. But with a rebuilt knee? I was not used to dealing with self-doubt. And the fact staring me in the face was simple: if this knee didn't heal up right, I was finished. I know those fears were rolling around in my mind and sometimes I just had to get away and clear my head. When I did, I would think about my dad working forty years in those coal mines, and that inspired me. A pro football player doesn't have much room to complain when you compare their work to a life in the coal mines. Remembering my dad's hard work always drove me back to rehab with a better attitude.

At the start of the 1985 season, the doctors and trainers insisted I wear a bulky knee brace all the time. I hated that thing. Dr. Scranton told me that he had fixed me physically, but I was going to have to do the work to recover mentally. After a big injury, he told me, there's a psychological dependence, a mental barrier. I think it might be especially true for a player who has to rely on speed and elusiveness. In an early game that season, I took a big hit right on the knee, so hard that it broke the brace. I think everybody was nervous about it, but I got up and I was okay. I ditched the brace, and from that point on, I felt I could run with the intensity I used to have. I rushed for more than one thousand yards that season, with forty-seven receptions, and was named the NFL's Comeback Player of the Year by *Sports Illustrated*.

Dr. Scranton told me that my operation had changed how knee surgeries were done for athletes. At the least, it changed the expectations for recovery from full ACL repairs. Up until then, ACL injuries almost always ended careers, particularly for running backs. I was the first who had been able to come back afterward and play at pretty much full capacity.

Everything for me and the Seahawks was completely back on track in 1986. We won ten games, and I rushed for nearly 1,500 yards. I was named second-team All-Pro that season and first-team All-Pro in 1987. There was satisfaction in knowing I could fight back from the injury, and also in knowing that for at least a while I was about as good as there was at the game's highest level. Those are the things you think about when your career is over.

In the end, the unrelenting violent collisions are what undoes a running back. I played great football for the Seahawks, but also had six operations (two on my knees and four on my ankles) while working for them, as well as multiple concussions. By 1988, I was twenty-seven, and my production was declining. After that season, the Seahawks didn't "protect" me on their roster, meaning I could be picked up as what the league referred to as a "Plan B free agent." As a result, the Los Angeles Rams signed me. I would have rather finished up in Seattle, so when the Seahawks didn't protect me on the roster, it was a deep disappointment.

It's a tough game—nobody will question that. And when your performance starts to decline, the game turns into a business in a hurry. Teams will hand you the pink slip when you're still a young man. That's the reality of the game. I lasted one season with the Rams after leaving Seattle, and it was suddenly over. It's hard to admit to yourself that you can't play anymore. The pride you take in your performance, the thing that drives you to get better, to excel, is exactly the thing that makes it hard for you to admit you're done. In my case, I never really decided it was time to retire. I wanted to keep playing if somebody would give me the chance. But you get the message pretty clearly when the phone stops ringing.

Seattle versus Miami, 1983.

CHAPTER 3

ON BENDED KNEE

1988–1991

ANA

My parents were such opposites. My dad spent most of his time on our large farm, where he was successful growing rice and beans. He loved the lifestyle in rural Brazil. My mother loved the city life at our home in Belo Horizonte (*Beautiful Horizon*), a six-hour drive away from the farm. While in the city, we had all the comforts of an upper-middle-class family: private school, maid, nanny, and for a while we even had a driver. We were privileged.

It was a very loving and close family despite having two homes so far apart. Mostly, we lived in the city, only going to the farm on vacations or holidays. It was the best of both worlds for us kids. My dad would take us hiking and teach us how to appreciate nature while my mom was always more of the intellectual type, really into reading and classical music. I fondly remember climbing onto my parents' bed, with my sister and my youngest brother, to listen to our parents tell stories of their own childhoods. They were such great storytellers, so animated and funny. Those were very special times that I treasured, and they shaped my image of an ideal family life.

Brazil is known for its party atmosphere, and that was the life I lived. Weekends were filled with late nights and a lot of partying. In South America, it's normal for young adult children to live with their parents until marriage, so I lived at home until I was twenty-six.

In 1985, I visited the USA for the first time. I was twenty-three, and I wanted to see more of the world. I had originally planned to go to England; I was into riding horses and thought it would be a good place for me. But a neighbor of mine had been in Seattle for a year working for an American-Brazilian family, and when her time was up, the family was interested in my coming to take her place. I put London on hold and headed to Seattle. I knew *almost* no English at all, and I nearly got lost in the New York and Minneapolis airports before finally reaching Seattle.

Once I got there, though, I loved Seattle, and I loved my job. I helped with household chores and babysitting in exchange for room and board. Life in America was different in so many ways. People were so respectful. I loved that. It wasn't always that way in Brazil. Sometimes a young woman might not feel safe in certain situations in Brazil. In Seattle, it was different. It was a kind of freedom I never had back home. I rode buses all over town and never had one problem. Being on my own, I learned a lot about myself. Having been pampered at home, I suddenly found that I loved doing things for myself: making my bed, doing my own laundry. It was the first time I was self-sufficient, and it felt good knowing I could take care of myself.

When the year in America was over, it was wonderful to go home and see my family again. But even though I had everything you could imagine in Brazil—family, comfort, a car, college, friends, and parties—I missed the independence I experienced in Seattle. I kept feeling that America was the place I was supposed to be. It was such a powerful emotion that I became depressed, and I stayed in that depression for two and a half years, with a constant voice inside me telling me to pack my bags and go back to Seattle.

Of course, there was a lot of pressure from my family to stay in Brazil, but it didn't feel like I fit in anymore. Brazil was the same, but I had changed. I had grown as a person, and I came to feel an important sense of self-worth and discipline in America. Even though I had been working as a house cleaner and I was riding the bus everywhere I went, I was respected. I loved it.

My feelings created conflicts between me and my family, though. I loved my family, but I felt more like myself in America. My mom didn't understand and went so far as to schedule an appointment with a therapist, hoping that he would talk me out of the idea of moving back to Seattle. He helped me clarify my thoughts and decide what was most important. Instead of talking me into staying, he looked at me and said, "It's time for you to cut the umbilical cord. You need to go live your own life."

A few months later, in 1989, I was off to America again. I had two suitcases, $600, and the determination that I was going to make it. There were so many unknowns, but I was excited and ready for whatever came my way. I again started cleaning houses and babysitting. It was hardly glamorous or well paying, but I was an independent woman. I was single and on my own in Seattle. I loved it. I missed that Brazilian sun, though. The gloomy weather took a while to get used to. Whenever it was nice, I would meet with a small group of friends from Brazil to get some sun at Green Lake. The Brazilian bikinis that were the style at home were apparently out of the ordinary in Seattle. They drew the attention of some guys who hung around at the lake. We learned that they were football players at the University of Washington. They were the first American football players I had come across, and my first impression wasn't entirely positive.

Through connections, I was introduced to a man who hired people to work as fragrance models in the department stores downtown. He thought I had a different look and sensed that my strong accent might attract customers. I was excited because the pay was good and it was a nice change from my other jobs. It was a strange life for a while; in the mornings I would clean houses, and in the afternoons I would get dressed up in heels and a fancy Christian Dior suit and head to the downtown Bon Marché. The job was to look classy and give out samples of Dior's Fahrenheit cologne. My English was limited at the time, so talking with people was a good learning experience for me.

One October afternoon, a man walked up to me. I was so taken by him I had to look away. I started blushing. I don't know what it was, maybe his smile, but truly, I'd never felt anything like that before. I actually went weak in the knees. I had heard people use that description of love at first sight. Maybe it's a cliché, but that's exactly what I felt. There was something deeper and more solid to it, though, more than just being swept off my feet by his looks. I could tell he had substance and confidence and was not just some guy hustling for a date. From the moment I met him, everything in my life changed. I knew this was it.

CURT

I always thought it was best to keep a low profile in public. I had a group of friends and we got together when there was time for it, but I wasn't a real partier or big into being out on the town. As an NFL player, I felt I had a responsibility to be a good citizen. If you played for the Seahawks, people in Seattle would recognize you; somebody was always watching, and there were people who might try to get you in bad situations that could endanger your career. Better to just not give them the opportunity.

Maybe I was too cautious in some ways. I didn't really date that much and was pretty shy around women. I came from that small town in West Virginia, and I'd always been so focused on football or training or schoolwork. I wasn't looking for a girlfriend. I certainly wasn't in the market for a wife, but one day while I was shopping in Bon Marché, a woman giving cologne samples definitely caught my eye. If I'd seen her on the street, yes, I would have looked, but I never would have had the nerve to stop and talk to her. It helped me that she was trying to sell me something. That made it easier for me to come up to her and start chatting.

Ana Teresa Mendes Costa was a very beautiful lady; she was dressed in this striking outfit, with her hair pulled back, so I couldn't help but notice her. I was going upstairs to the men's department when I saw her, and I just had to stop and try a sample. Her accent was really interesting, but her personality was what really kept my attention. There was just so much about her. She was new to America and knew nothing about football, and she had absolutely no idea who I was. I liked that.

I walked away with cologne and her phone number.

Conversations with Ana were tougher on the phone; I had a really hard time understanding her because of the accent. Still, the first time I called, we talked for almost an hour. I had avoided telling her what I did for a living several times, but I finally had to tell her. "I play football." She shot right back, "If you think you're impressing me with that, you're wrong."

She told me her impression of football players. Totally stereotypical. Totally negative. I liked her style, though, and wasn't offended. (Did I mention she was very beautiful?) I stood up for myself and convinced her I wasn't some big dumb athlete.

We arranged a date. And it was awful. Really, really awful. Our relationship came close to a quick and very disappointing ending. I took her to a Seattle club, Jazz Alley, which seemed like a good idea, but it was so packed and so loud we couldn't even talk. We were kind of just standing there and yelling at each other over the music every now and then. Her English was hard to understand even in a quiet room, so it was a terrible place for a first date. I had to do something; this was going nowhere. I was ready to cut my losses and take her home, but she was like nobody I'd ever known—her looks, her voice, that accent—and that was enough to keep me from tossing in the towel. I went to the pay phone and called my friend Harold Reynolds, an infielder for the Seattle Mariners. I told him about this woman who was terrific, but we just weren't connecting the way I'd hoped. He told me to stay where I was because he'd be right over.

Harold saw that nobody could communicate in that place. So he pulled us out of there and took us to a quiet restaurant in Bellevue. Harold's wisdom really helped us break the ice, and once Ana and I started talking, I told him he could leave. Harold saved the day.

Ana started coming to Seahawks games with a friend named Raul Palacios to watch me play. He was from Uruguay and was a PhD student at the University of Washington. He'd lived in Brazil for a time and spoke Portuguese, so he could explain the rules and strategy of football to her. After the games, we'd go out for a nice dinner. She was very surprised by what it was like to be out in public with a professional athlete. I always appreciated fans who cared enough to ask for autographs or share their enthusiasm for my play. I would sign anything they wanted me to. It's a part of the job, a privilege, really, to be in that position, but it was hard for her to get used to our meals being interrupted so often.

We both knew how much we meant to each other as that autumn wore on, but our relationship was suddenly put in jeopardy by the forces of bureaucracy. I didn't know it at the time, but Ana was having problems with her visa. She came to Seattle in the spring of 1989 on a six-month visa. It had almost expired. She applied for an extension and was denied with no reasons given. She didn't want me to feel pressured in our relationship, so she never told me about it. She mentioned it to her friend Heather Moyer, wife of my teammate Paul Moyer. Of course, Heather told Paul, and Paul told me.

The threat of her having to leave the country was a game changer for me. I had to examine how much she truly meant to me. We had a serious talk and realized that neither of us wanted her to go back to Brazil. With this relationship, we'd found something special that we didn't want to let go of. I talked to some of the Seahawks' front office people about her visa situation, and it turned out they had some pretty powerful connections. Eventually, Senator Slade Gorton got involved and obtained an extension that gave me enough time to ask her a very important question.

I hatched a plan for Valentine's Day, 1990. It was before I was picked up by the LA Rams. I had bought an engagement ring and made a reservation for us at the revolving restaurant at the top of the Space Needle. Mr. Romance, right? It was a rare snowy night in Seattle, and it made the view up there amazing, with all the city lights twinkling through the falling snow. I set it up so the waiter would start us off with champagne. I gave him the ring and had him put it in Ana's glass. The drinks came and we were talking and talking, and Ana just kept sipping and sipping as I watched her. Somehow, she finished the drink without noticing the ring. Maybe she thought there was ice in her champagne? I finally had to tell her to look *in* the glass.

When she saw the engagement ring in the bottom, I got down on one knee, and when she said yes, the whole restaurant started cheering. I didn't know it, but everybody in the place must have been watching. It sounded like Seahawks fans doing the wave in the Kingdome after a touchdown.

The timing of Ana's coming into my life was perfect. I needed her; I just didn't know how much. Back then, nobody prepared players to handle the twilight of their career. That's why so many players got into deep financial troubles and had such a hard time dealing with the transition to life after the NFL. Here's how it goes for a lot of players: All of a sudden, you're not identified as a professional football player, which was an identity that had served you well. You have to be able to create a new identity—at age thirty. When you're not on the field with your teammates every day, you lose touch with those close friends. And all that camaraderie that was so rewarding is gone. Ana helped me through those difficult transitions.

I was fortunate in my retirement, beyond having found Ana. For so long a player's life is regimented by others. Somebody from the team would tell you where you had to be, at what time, and what you needed to do. They didn't want you having to think about anything but winning football games. As a result, a nice paycheck got funneled into your account. What's not to love about that? As a retiree, though, you're suddenly on your own. A lot of guys have trouble with that. A lot of them find their marriages suffering. Thankfully, I had Ana and would be starting my new life, *our* new life, together. I had invested well and benefited from good advisers while I was a player. I had the time and the means, so I didn't want to just lend my name to a business, I wanted to get totally involved in a new career.

In 1991, I went through the National Automobile Dealers Association training program and eventually acquired a Buick/Pontiac/GMC dealership in the Seattle suburb of Bellevue. To me, business felt like sports in some ways. I had a plan, and I executed it by involving my personnel and knowing my product. I worked hard at becoming a good businessman. I focused on what I needed to do and communicated with my employees. I wasn't just a figurehead; I was running the show, and it was important to me that I be totally involved. I think the dealership capitalized on the recognition I had as a former Seahawks player, sure, but that wasn't the only reason it was successful.

We had a financial foundation in place, and Ana and I were rock solid in our relationship. We knew we were blessed, and I'm sure we thought we were ready for anything. Sometimes I look back and remember what coach Chuck Knox said to the team so many times. He told us that you had to be ready and able to adapt to your circumstances. Often, that's what separates winning teams from losing teams. Things can change drastically at any time, so, he would say, you have to be able "to play the hand you're dealt."

Very true, Coach. I thought about that warning often in the years that followed.

CHAPTER 4

RYAN WARNER NEVER CRIED

October 1991

ANA

We did all the things most parents do when they're expecting their first child, making our home a welcoming place for a new little person. We put together the crib and painted the nursery. My mother and sister were coming to Seattle to help out with the baby, and this would be like a reunion as well as a celebration of a new life. We had the typical baby shower with all the usual presents and well-wishes from friends.

It was a very joyful time. Curt had played his last season in the NFL, and we decided to move from LA back to our condo in Kirkland, just east of Seattle. So many of Curt's friends and old teammates were still in Seattle, and that's where his best business contacts would be. His reputation and name recognition there were still really strong, and it was the first place I'd lived in America, so it felt like going home for both of us. It was where we planned to plant our roots.

Retirement was a hard transition for Curt in some ways, and I was sympathetic, but I also had seen how painful the game had been for him. So, honestly, I was glad he wouldn't be going through the physical beating anymore. As a wife, it had been frightening to watch my husband play in professional football games. Every player on the other team was trying to hurt him. He would get hit almost every play by so many men. I'd cringe and hold my breath until I saw him get up. Every time he walked back to the huddle, I watched to see if he was limping. It was nerve-racking. I know it's part of why fans love football, but it's hard for a player's wife to watch.

Curt always played so hard; it didn't matter how many people hit him, he still kept trying to gain yards. He was so determined, he'd keep running until there was a whole pile of massive men pulling him down. Sometimes I'd just cover my eyes. After games, he was often so bruised, or sometimes cut and bandaged up. He'd have injuries he didn't even know about until after the game, maybe even the next morning. And there were injuries he didn't even bother to tell me about. That is how football players are. It's part of the culture. But even for fit and strong men who are used to getting beaten up, the cumulative effect is enormous. When he realized it was over, we were both ready to get on with the next chapter of our lives. Having children and building a family was important to both of us, and after we moved back to Seattle, we wanted to get started right away.

Our first pregnancy went perfectly. Of course, we were so excited. In fact, the baby had grown so well that he was very large. As we were nearing the due date, the doctor started considering a C-section delivery, so we went in for a final ultrasound exam to check everything and make a decision on how to deliver. The baby seemed less active; he'd been a kicker and then he wasn't. I assumed it was a matter of positioning, and with him being so large, things were getting tight in there.

As he had been for every examination, Curt was at my side. I had the natural anxieties of any mother nearing her first delivery. Curt always got me to relax by kidding with me or the doctors—keeping things light while also being very attentive and involved. This time was no different. After all those months of pregnancy and anticipation, the reality hit that it might be only a short time before we finally would meet our baby. It was a mixture of excitement with the natural fear of the unknown.

I watched Curt's face during the exam. I had found this comforting during past appointments. The doctor started listening with his stethoscope, moving it around my belly. Slowly at first, and then quicker. Curt's face seemed to grow anxious, his eyes widening. The doctor went back over my belly again. This exam was in his office, but after another pass around with the stethoscope, the doctor said he thought we should go across the street to Evergreen Hospital for a better look at things. I didn't even consider that there might be a problem. Maybe we were going there to use better examination tools.

Once they got me in a room, he looked at the baby with an ultrasound. During most of these exams, doctors would give us a running commentary about the baby's progress, but the doctor was quiet as he moved his instrument. Still looking at Curt's face for comfort, I could tell he felt this was going differently from other exams. I don't know how long it took for the doctor to determine what he was seeing on the ultrasound screen, but it seemed like forever.

The doctor looked up and told us that the baby had gone silent since our last exam. The words seemed vague. *Silent* could mean resting or sleeping, or whatever babies do to prepare for being born. But the look on the doctor's face told the story.

He clarified. The baby, he said, had died.

I just couldn't believe him. It had to be a mistake. Mistakes happen all the time. The baby was ready, everything had been perfect at our last exam, all the tests had positive outcomes. I wanted him to keep looking. If he would keep looking, surely he'd see whatever he needed to see and apologize for questioning the baby's health.

No, he was clear, our baby would be stillborn. What an awful word.

I insisted he do a C-section. Get the baby out. I wanted the baby out. I was sure the baby needed to get out. In my mind, if the baby was out of me, he could start breathing and would be all right. The doctor told us that it was better for me, and my recovery, if the baby was delivered naturally. He said he would induce labor the following morning. It would give us time to get our heads around the reality of our situation.

We went home. Curt and I were in complete disbelief. We really didn't talk about it; instead, we went on acting as if the baby were still alive in me. My mother and my sister were on their plane from Brazil, so I couldn't get hold of them. My friend Raul was going to pick them up at the airport. I couldn't imagine them getting off the plane to the news that we'd lost our baby. I couldn't think clearly about what was happening. How would we spend that evening with them? We were saved from that difficult scenario when, within an hour of getting home, I began having contractions. We raced back to the hospital.

I believed—truly believed—through every minute of that delivery that our baby would be safe and well. No matter what the doctor had told us. No matter what the ultrasound had shown earlier that day.

When Ryan was delivered, I didn't breathe for a long, desperate moment. I was focusing all my concentration on willing him to cry. *Cry, please!* I prayed there had been a mistake. I was sure he'd cry. Being delivered would be what he needed, to get out and breathe air. *Dear*

God, let him cry. I kept waiting for a miracle, but there was just empty silence.

Ryan never cried.

They cleaned him up and brought him to us. The delivery room was emptied to allow us private time with our son. It was all the time we were going to get with our little Ryan. He looked so perfect. A perfect child who never cried.

Curt became so upset. I couldn't calm him, so I called a nurse to come and take Ryan away. Curt and I stayed together in that room in the maternity ward that night, crying and hugging, trying to convince each other that we'd be all right as we listened to the wails of healthy babies up and down the hall of the maternity ward.

The doctor told us that Ryan's umbilical cord had probably become pinched in the days leading up to that final appointment. It's rare, but it happens. Ryan was totally healthy in all other regards. Nine pounds, one ounce at full term. To be told your baby is dead and to still have to go through labor and delivery seemed like some kind of sadistic punishment on top of the tragedy. I had gone through all the classes and read the books that expecting mothers read, and never was there a mention that the baby might die. It's unthinkable. When it happened to us, the shock was indescribable.

I had always looked forward to that joyful moment when I'd be wheeled out of the hospital with a new baby in my arms. I've heard mothers describe the birth of their first child as the day you enter a new stage of life, when you suddenly forget what life had been like before you had a baby.

But what now? What happens when that day goes wrong?

Maybe it's accepted protocol in such cases, or just their remarkably kind instincts, but before the nurses wheeled me out of the hospital the morning we were to go home, they gave me a small stuffed bear to hold. They knew that no mother imagines herself leaving the hospital empty-handed. It was something to hold, to focus on. Those nurses never knew how much that little bear helped me get from that hospital bed to the car, where we would start finding ways to deal with our grief.

My mother and sister were at our home, and they'd offered to take care of clearing away the baby things from the nursery. It was sweet, but I asked them not to. Curt and I had put everything together in that room, and it just seemed that we should share the dismantling of the crib, the taking down of the decorations, the packing up of the shower gifts, too. I thought maybe if we did it together, it would feel like a tribute of some kind, a part of the healing process for both of us. Closure, perhaps. But there never really is closure to losing your child. Curt couldn't go into the nursery for a long time. I'd sneak into the room when Curt wasn't around, to sit alone and rock in the chair where I expected to nurse Ryan. I rocked and cried a great deal in that chair.

Reminders were everywhere. I didn't think it could hurt so much to see pregnant women or mothers with their babies. We had a friend who had a baby shortly after Ryan was born. It was a boy. I convinced myself the baby looked like Ryan. I had a very hard time looking at that baby without breaking down. Our friend's child was two years old before I could see him without it triggering fresh mourning for Ryan. I knew other children had nothing to do with what happened to Ryan, but the hurt was there anyway, and for a while, I had to turn away from mothers with babies. We'd get invited to parties, and if the family had children, we'd find reasons to stay away.

It was hard to even know what my emotions were. Envy of other parents? Confusion about what they did right that I didn't? Heartache? Grief? Surely. I knew I could never get over these feelings. Not an hour went by when I wasn't saddened by the thoughts of losing Ryan.

I had seen how strong Curt had been through the end of his football career, how squared away he always had been emotionally, and how he dealt with physical pain without ever complaining. I knew he was made of some kind of inner steel, but this loss affected him so deeply. That night in the hospital, after the nurses had taken Ryan away, it seemed like the one thing in our lives we could count on was that we were together, there for each other. It was a certainty we each could carry with us. Our love for one another was forged and tempered to an even greater strength and depth through the experience.

Curt worked at being strong for my sake. It was his perspective that helped me start to cope with the heartache. He told me, "Ryan belonged to the Lord first, and from the start, he was His, not ours." It was the first small dose of comfort on the long road to healing.

That's why Ryan's gravestone, in a cemetery in Bellevue, Washington, reads: "The Lord giveth, the Lord taketh away. Blessed be the name of the Lord." (Job 1:21)

He is buried with the small stuffed bear the nurses gave me that sad morning.

CURT

I tried to be prepared for everything, but I hadn't considered this. You can't prepare for a baby dying. Everybody knows that when you go to the hospital, you bring home a baby. But we didn't. Ryan was our son, and he was perfect, a big, healthy baby boy, but for whatever reason, the good Lord decided to keep him. That's how we chose to look at it.

For months, something as simple as a wrong word could bring Ana or me to tears. I'd lost both my parents by then, but this felt so different. It was so unnatural. Parents are supposed to go before their children.

Everywhere I'd go, I would see families together, parents with their kids. I didn't even notice them before I became a parent. But I noticed every single one after that. Every time I saw a family with a little one, I'd guess the age of the baby and imagine what Ryan would have looked like at that age. Something about picturing him growing made him seem more alive, even if just in my imagination. But it was painful.

Ana and I were both devastated, but she was stronger than I was. I learned to cope a little better, gradually, or maybe I just got a little better at hiding the pain. There's some value in that, too.

Ana wanted to have another child as soon as possible. I understood what was in her heart and why trying again seemed like the best thing, so I went along with her on it because she needed that to move on. But, really, I was worried there'd just be a lot more pain. Even now, after all this time, it is hard to cope with the loss of Ryan. He wasn't with us long, but he was our child.

Austin, Jonathan, and Christian.

CHAPTER 5

THE WARNER BOYS

1991–1999

ANA

We weren't going to give up on trying to have a family, we both agreed on that. In fact, I wanted to have a baby as soon as possible. Maybe I was trying to cover the pain of Ryan's loss. But it didn't work out that way.

Perhaps my body wasn't ready. Maybe your body knows when your life is out of balance. Whatever the reasons, one miscarriage followed another, and our grief compounded. There were high hopes followed by deep pain. So many things went through my head, and I was left trying to fight off the sense of futility. Mostly, I just wondered why. Why us? What did we do? What did *I* do?

After the loss of one of the pregnancies, they told me it wasn't really a baby. Still, the pain of losing what we thought was a baby was very real to us. We then lost another baby early on. I don't remember how far along it was. I know these things happen, but so often? I was turning into an emotional mess; I kept thinking that getting pregnant was going to be the answer. But each failed attempt or miscarriage only added more pain. It felt like I had a hole in my heart. It was as if I could actually feel it, physically—an ache in my chest.

I wanted kids—we wanted kids—and I was growing afraid I'd never have a child. Finally, I was pregnant again, and though obviously I was at a high risk, things seemed to be going well. The doctors were tracking the progress with regular ultrasound exams and repeatedly measuring the levels of amniotic fluid. Maybe it was superstition, or we were just trying to avoid triggering bad memories, but we didn't prepare the baby's room this time, and we didn't allow friends to throw us a baby shower even as I neared full term. We didn't even put together the crib before we left for the hospital.

It was a long, stressful nine months, and as we neared the final days, fears dominated my thoughts. This baby was a large boy, as Ryan had been, and doctors scheduled an early inducement at thirty-eight weeks. Curt and I focused on every beep of the baby's heart monitor, and our second baby boy was born. When Curt and I heard him howl, it brought us both to tears. Our son was alive and well, beautiful and healthy. We named him Jonathan because it means "God's gift."

Jonathan's infancy was a magical time, a time of great healing for us. We were so encouraged by how well things were going that nine months later we were pregnant again. It seemed like a great way to celebrate our success. We finally did it right, so we tried again.

During our ten-week sonogram, Curt thought he saw something on the monitor and asked, "What's it look like when there are twins?" The doctor just laughed and dismissed the question as obvious. "We'd see two babies."

Two weeks later, the ultrasound tech had barely started the scan when she said, "Has the doctor talked to you?"

"Is there something wrong?" I asked, frightened to the core. "Tell me, tell me what's wrong!"

"No . . . no . . . nothing's wrong, but dear, you're having twins," the tech said. I took a deep breath to calm myself and then looked up and started laughing. "Lord, you sure have some sense of humor." We had prayed so hard for one child, and we were getting two more. Our family was now growing as if making up for lost time.

Of course we monitored this pregnancy carefully every step of the way. The ultrasounds soon started showing that Baby A had begun exerting dominance over Baby B, absorbing more than its half of the nutrients. The doctors said it was not uncommon with twins, who tend to compete in utero, but if the imbalance continued, it could get to the point where Baby B might fail before birth. As the doctor told us about it, I could only focus on the loss of another child. But Baby B, Christian, was a fighter, and rallied hard in the latter stages of the pregnancy. Christian started out as an underdog, and he's fought through so many things ever since. We love that quality in him so much.

I gained seventy pounds with the twins, and both ended up developing on schedule despite Austin's initial dominance. Austin (six and a half pounds) was born before Christian (six pounds) in a joyfully uncomplicated delivery. My mother and a friend were there to help when we brought the boys home. The nursery at our home was suddenly very crowded.

I started feeling like I was a human Dairy Queen, breastfeeding two babies, with eighteen-month-old Jonathan running around in the energetic way that eighteen-month-olds do. It didn't take long before I felt myself wearing down. With the rapid-fire pregnancies and the pressure of caring for three small humans, I felt like I was spinning. Beyond exhausted, I wasn't getting enough sleep, and I had no time to recuperate. My life was overwhelming me. It's likely that I never really regained emotional stability after the loss of Ryan, which was probably compounded by the miscarriages that followed. My life went from one heartache to another for so long, and suddenly I had everything multiplied by three in the span of a year and a half. At times, I would just start crying. I wasn't sure what it was like to feel normal. To feel like myself—the person I was before I had become pregnant with Ryan. I had lost that sense of who I was.

I was diagnosed with postpartum depression.

Curt saw how I was struggling and jumped in, volunteering to take the night shifts so I could at least catch up on some rest. For months he lived on very little sleep except the quick catnaps on the couch in his office at the car dealership. I don't know how he ran his business without getting sleep, but he managed, showing the same kind of determination I had seen him capable of on the football field.

Allowing an exhausted person to rest is one of the greatest gifts imaginable. I was in such need of help at that point that Curt's dedication felt heroic. It wasn't just his sharing of the workload but his generosity of spirit and his positive attitude. I knew he was exhausted, too, but he never complained and never "kept score" as couples so often do. Frequently my sleep was uneasy, because of all the anxiety, but whenever I got any rest, it felt glorious.

We also were getting greatly appreciated help from "Grandma Hutcherson"—Hulia Mae Hutcherson, the mother of our pastor in Seattle, Ken Hutcherson. She loved the boys, calling them "little rascals." She helped out as their nanny when the twins were very young and we were still living in Kirkland, and after we moved to Camas, she would often take the train down and stay for stretches of several days at a time. People who help you when you're most in need are the friends you never forget. Her help was truly significant since we had no family in the area, and for so much of the time we were simply on our own.

When the twins neared two years old, though, their usual bouts of crying grew more intense and more frequent. Almost menacing. I was beginning to worry that something more might be affecting their moods. Christian, especially, was sick all the time. It seemed like he always had ear infections or sinus infections. We were constantly going to see pediatricians. When we took the twins to one of Curt's doctors, he diagnosed them both with pica, a mineral-deficiency disorder, and blood tests revealed an iron deficiency. We began giving the twins vitamins and supplements to treat pica, but the behaviors continued to become more extreme. Pica couldn't be the only issue. Sometimes doctors thought they had answers, but they usually led to more questions, deeper frustrations, and worsening behaviors. And every unproductive doctor's appointment made it all seem more mysterious.

We spent three years going to countless appointments with various doctors and specialists, and we tried just about anything they suggested. But the twins' level of discomfort and unhappiness continued to grow. I've heard that parents often feel a sickness of their own when their children are hurting. I know I did. Every day that the boys dealt with these troubles was a day we hurt along with them. The doubts and confusion started consuming our lives.

CURT

In sports you scout your opponent, you understand their strengths and weaknesses. You form a game plan to exploit your advantages. But what happens when you know so little about what you're heading into, and even as you learn more, it seems like the situation is constantly changing, with new theories making everything harder to understand?

We went to the experts and we trusted them. But when there's something obviously wrong and nobody can tell you anything, the frustration just builds. Later, one of the twins' doctors told us that identifying autism characteristics sometimes presents a "moving target," and he was right—that's exactly what it felt like. Always changing, sometimes hard to find.

Being from an athletic background, I understood that things happen to our bodies and doctors are there to help you recover. So I have great respect for the practice of medicine and for doctors. They sustained and prolonged my football career. But if you don't know something, you just don't know it, and when it came to the twins, it seemed like everybody was guessing.

It was like some huge puzzle. I tried to focus on the things that I knew and could understand. One of the few things that I knew for certain was that my wife was exhausted. She was getting worn out by everything. Three little boys are a lot for anybody, but when the twins started becoming harder to deal with, our lives got so much more complicated.

We tried everything we could imagine. Doctor after doctor. We weren't arriving at the root of it, but I tried to learn more at every exam. So often when we'd go to an exam, they had evaluation charts telling you the stages of normal development—what kids should be doing at certain ages. I'd look at those and tell the doctors, Our guys are doing none of these things. Why? They're way behind what Jonathan was doing at their age. Why? They aren't acting the same, either, and there has to be something that is causing them to be behind. What is it? We went to a speech pathologist because the twins were falling so far behind on their language skills. She seemed angry at us that they weren't more developed. What were we supposed to do? All we could think was to see more doctors. Ask more questions. Keep searching for answers.

It was toughest on Ana. Because she was at home with them every day, she bore the weight of it. She'd been through so much already and was so worn down from the pregnancies. She needed to get some rest, and I had to take some of the load off her. It became a challenge to try to keep everything in place. When I was at the dealership, I would shift into work mode and try to be as efficient as I could be, to make the most of every minute. When a business has your name on it, it's very personal and a matter of pride to make it successful. I had a family to support and a business to run, but there was never any doubt what my top priority was.

I had this feeling that when we finally found out what was wrong, it would all seem obvious. In none of those many doctors' appointments over several years, leading up to our appointment with the doctor in Portland, did anybody ever even use the word *autism*. Not once. With what we know about factors that contribute to diagnoses now, it seems astonishing it was never caught. We don't blame anybody for it. That's just how it was. They didn't know.

CHAPTER 6

NOW WHAT?

1999–2007

ANA

Back in the '90s, autism awareness was lacking—even in the medical profession. Age five is now, in most cases, considered a late diagnosis. Or toward the latter end of being ideal. There's no way to know how much Austin and Christian would have benefited from a quicker diagnosis and an earlier regimen of aggressive treatment. Some specialists have told us that early treatment tends to be more effective, as children's brains are still a great deal more malleable. Communication, particularly, is supposed to be enhanced by early interventions. Once we finally knew what we were up against, we wanted to attack it with everything we had. I felt like I had to personally find a cure. If it was a matter of strength of will and hard work, I was going to do it. I was going to fix them. My sons deserved that kind of effort from their mother. I just wasn't sure how we needed to go about it. Stepping into the world of autism was like trying to find our way in a dark room. And I wasn't interested in tiptoeing around until we got our bearings. The twins had been diagnosed late, and we needed to try to play catch-up the best we could.

I dived into research and discovered hundreds of theories. But very few included concrete facts and scientific evidence. Being diagnosed with health problems can be difficult in almost any case. But most of the time, the sufferer learns there are accepted treatments, time lines, and protocols. Not with ASD, not back then. I went back to one of the doctors we'd seen before the diagnosis, to check the boys' records for any clues we might have missed. Was there something that was seen then that might help us in approaching their treatments going forward? It turned out that the doctor had charted nothing about the possibility of the boys having autism, but had diagnosed me with post-traumatic stress disorder—without ever mentioning it to me.

While I started really revving up to take on this autism challenge, Curt was mostly quiet and reserved. He processes things so differently. He likes to think before he acts. I resented that way of coping with the situation. I was like, *Come on, we've got to fight!* He was holding things in. It caused some troubles for us. I was so upset. I was angry, and I wanted him to be as angry as I was. I kept wondering why he wasn't getting worked up. I knew he loved the boys and was sick about this.

I was so determined to fix it—right now. *Get out of my way, I've got work to do!* I became a drill sergeant, barking orders, and I didn't care if I was hurting whoever was in my way. Sometimes Curt would try to calm me down, and I knew he was trying to help, but his calmness made me angry, too. We decided to go to counseling. We sat down with our pastor, Dr. Ken "Hutch" Hutcherson, and he talked to us about finding ways to deal with our life. I had to learn to understand how Curt processes things. He had a lot going on inside that he didn't want anybody to know about. Even me. Fair enough, I had feelings I wasn't telling him about, too.

Of course he cared about the twins as much as I did. Of course he was frustrated and angry. He was just as upset as I was, he just didn't show it the way I did. I felt his demeanor had something to do with his toughness, his manliness. I knew how he was raised. I knew what he was like when he played football. I came to understand that mostly he was trying to settle me down; he knew that if he got worked up, it probably would have just fueled my anger more. I had been so single-minded in my own approach that I didn't really understand how much emotion was stewing inside him.

I feel awful about the way I acted and about some of the things I said to him. I am absolutely sure there were many times when other husbands would have up and left. I was that pushy and insistent, and not very sensitive to his feelings. This would have been hard on any couple. Extremely hard. But Curt kept his cool. Curt had unbelievable patience with me, with all of us. I think maybe the best thing about going to Hutch for help was that it caused Curt to open up a little. That was good for both of us.

As he had when we were first married, Hutch stressed communication as the key to a good marriage. We always had our love and never questioned that. But we needed to communicate better. Learning to read and support each other ultimately helped us deal with the challenges we faced then and in later years. It was probably the sort of advice that many counselors would give about new marriages and parenting, but it reached us.

CURT

I kept getting hung up on what the doctor said: "There's nothing you can do." I had trouble handling that kind of attitude. That language seemed like a personal challenge.

I kept going back to that diagnosis. After Ana started researching, we knew the doctor was right: it had to be autism. But the doctor couldn't be right about what it meant for the twins' future. We didn't understand the range of ASD, just how broad that spectrum is. It took us a while to learn that it isn't a one-size-fits-all diagnosis.

I don't like uncertainty, especially when it involves my family, my children—people I love more than anything in the world. I got quiet after the diagnosis. I'm not a person who rages or screams or swears. It wasn't that I was down or defeated, but I had to sort through it all, to start building up a level of knowledge and understanding. That took some time.

At first, it sounded to me like the twins had been handed a life sentence. I thought that maybe the "nothing can be done" comment meant that we could never expect them to progress, that they'd stay at this level of development even as they became full-grown men. I didn't know enough about autism initially. I know, at times, I looked at it from the wrong perspective: I thought way too often about how these boys would be viewed by others. I was worried that they wouldn't be judged as normal. I pretty quickly realized that what others thought was not very important. Keeping the twins safe and as healthy as possible had to become our primary focus.

Being parents to three young boys is demanding on its own. The autism diagnosis added so many more concerns that it was hard for me to get my head around it all. Suddenly, Ana and I were considering various treatments and medications and supplements on a weekly basis. We were trying to make important decisions about the health and future of our children at a time when we had little more than a superficial understanding of their condition.

Ana and I dealt with this early phase of our experience very differently. Ana thought I had closed up, emotionally. Maybe she read that as withdrawing, or not being as supportive as I could be. Sometimes I thought back to the times in football when it felt like chaos and I just needed to call a time-out to get everything in order. Everybody needs time like that to catch their breath and get their wits about them. But there were no time-outs in the lives we were leading. No halftimes. This was something we were going to face all day, every day.

Ana was going one hundred miles an hour in every direction. I knew managing this diagnosis wasn't going to be simple or easy. The doctors had made it clear this was going to be a long-haul deal. Going at that pace didn't seem sustainable, but she was eager to try everything, examine every option. Seriously, I believed that if she heard somebody had helped cure their kids by putting an elephant in their backyard, she would start insisting we figure out a way to get an elephant. Sometimes I'd try to pull her back a little, maybe not jump into some treatment she read about on the internet. Maybe I wasn't convinced it was the right thing to do, or maybe it didn't seem legit. But Ana was driven by pure emotion, and sometimes I just didn't think that was being rational. That was probably what caused our friction. I thought we needed to be more cautious about which methods of treatment we were trying out on our sons, and that we shouldn't just rush blindly down some of these paths. But Ana was like a mother grizzly bear whose cubs were threatened. She was going to fight back with everything she had. Most of the time, I would listen and go along with her plans. I'd allow her to vent when she got angry or emotional. This was my wife, and I saw how much she was hurting. I was worried that the pace she was on was going to burn her out.

Sometimes she would lash out at me, and I had to say, Wait, hold on a second, that's out of line. Sometimes I had to hold my ground because getting after me wasn't going to do either of us any good. I wasn't the opposition—we were on the same team. It wasn't ever throwing plates or anything like that; she was just so intense about everybody following the exact protocols for treatments. When we didn't, we heard about it. One time she said she knew she was giving orders like a sergeant, so I called her "Sergeant Warner" and saluted. I was joking, but that's what she was like when she was giving orders. And then she laughed. I think.

I believe that part of her being so driven was because she couldn't get over the false notion that this was somehow her fault. I had to keep reminding her that the doctors said this diagnosis had nothing to do with her. Convincing her of that might have been the most important thing I could do. I know she appreciated hearing it from me. But deep down, I don't think she really believed me.

I never wanted to get into the blame game. You can't blame the other one for anything—not for the cause of it, not for the frustrations. Nothing. That never helps. Nobody has a magic wand and the power to determine what's going to happen to your children. Autism happened to us, and what we went through during those years after the diagnosis could tear any couple apart, no question. We both knew that, and we talked about it very seriously. We were committed to working through everything together.

One thing I believed was that we couldn't start throwing ourselves a pity party. Spending time saying "woe is us" would get us nowhere. We had to rely on each other. I knew that if I let myself get down, then there would be no one to take care of Ana. I couldn't be any help to her or the boys if I collapsed or decided I didn't want this life any longer. Ana suggested that perhaps we talk with our pastor, Dr. Ken Hutcherson, to work through how frustrated we had become. He had always been a great counselor to us, wise and helpful. Still, I wasn't comfortable at all with the idea of talking to Pastor Hutch about our troubles. At the time, I thought that a man doesn't deal with his troubles by talking about them. Nobody in my family ever talked about their troubles with anyone outside the family. My parents had great, deep conversations all the time. They went through so much when I was young, but they didn't go around telling people how hard their lives were. I was raised understanding that you don't complain. Complaining didn't do anyone any good. You don't ever quit, and you don't ever complain. That was just not something a man did.

Hutch was a wonderful, gentle man, and he had been an NFL linebacker, so he was pretty imposing. He helped change what I thought it meant to be a "real man."

CHAPTER 7

FIGHTING BACK

ANA

The internet became my classroom and my library, and more importantly, my community. I discovered so many people gathering in this electronic village to share ideas and information about autism. There is a real people-helping-people quality to many of the message boards and chat sites. So often, I found links to medical websites and news of current developments in autism, but maybe more valuable than information was the realization that so many people were willing to offer support to others who were also fighting the fight.

Initially, there was comfort in just knowing we weren't alone in this strange new world of ASD. Mostly, this community was a place where parents offered suggestions on what had worked with their children and what hadn't. At times I was excited to hear of possible new treatments that somebody was trying, and at other times I was disappointed when a parent warned that something else was a waste of time. It was obvious that some people had a tougher time with autism than others, and I thought we all benefited from being in touch with those sympathetic to our troubles.

After I told the story of how the twins had started damaging our house by kicking holes in the walls—many holes, all over the house—a mother told of a minor disaster with her son, who had plugged a bathroom sink, turned on the water, and inexplicably left the room. The flooding caused thousands of dollars of damage. I offered my sympathy and kept mindful of that as another source of havoc that my boys might discover. The stories weren't always relevant to the behaviors I would see with my own children, but they reminded me to stay vigilant. It kept my mind open to possibilities I would otherwise never anticipate.

One thing that struck me very early in my participation in these online discussions was how appropriate the name "autism spectrum disorder" is. There is such a broad range of conditions and symptoms with this developmental and neurological disorder. A popular saying of those online is: "If you meet one child with autism, you know about one child with autism." The difference in the range of abilities on the spectrum can be enormous from child to child, so it's important not to make blanket statements about people with the disorder. Those diagnosed with ASD may be low functioning and entirely nonverbal or may have very high intellects but have some problems dealing with other aspects of their lives, such as social situations. This all constitutes a very big umbrella, which makes it so hard to find treatments that work consistently for everybody. It's also why there's so little consensus among people trying to find ways to deal with children on different points of the spectrum.

I learned that I couldn't just rely on the notion that because something worked for someone else's child it would work for mine. In some cases, the same treatment might have a very different effect. Plus, our boys were changing so often that new behaviors were coming at us constantly, forcing us to modify our approach sometimes before we could even determine if the last thing we tried was working. It was like trying to put together a jigsaw puzzle with the added challenge of having the pieces always changing size and shape.

Shortly after the twins' diagnosis, doctors gave us a short list of other parents in our region who would be willing to share their experiences with autism. Curt phoned a woman on the list, Helyn Rosemurgy, who helped us get in touch with a small army of therapists that had been effective in treating her son. It was the first time we heard of anything meaningful and productive being done for kids like Austin and Christian. Meeting Helyn was like finding a pathfinder into unknown territory. She showed me a video on Applied Behavior Analysis (ABA) created by Dr. O. Ivar Lovaas, which emphasized early and intensive behavioral therapy. She introduced me to her son and told me how effective the ABA therapy had been for him.

Her son was a little younger than Austin and Christian, but he was at about the same level of development as our boys. Dr. Lovaas had a clinic in Portland at the time, where he was starting a pilot program for ABA therapy. We decided to give ABA a try, and within the first couple of weeks after diagnosis, the twins were enrolled in the program. We started feeling such a sense of progress. It was as if we were finally able to do something that would make the boys better. We started hearing a wonderful word: *recovery*. We were encouraged and hopeful for the first time in years.

Suddenly, our house was invaded by an army of therapists. We put together a team of therapists that shuffled back and forth to our house for treatments that filled forty hours a week for each boy. There was a constant rotation of therapists every couple hours who would use flash cards to help develop language and positive reinforcement to shape behavior. It was an intense environment. There were people in our home all the time. I could barely keep track of everybody coming and going. To make sure we stayed organized and on schedule, we had meetings with all the therapists once a week to compare notes on progress and treatments.

The chaos was productive. The boys learned a lot; we were seeing meaningful results. They were recognizing numbers and letters and even starting to read a little. Their progress was so promising. We finally felt we were on the right track.

The boys were supposed to start kindergarten in September of 1999. We invited the school district's special education director to our house to meet the boys and observe the work they were doing with the therapists. At that time, though, the school district did not have classroom placement appropriate for the boys' level of development, so the school's director approved our applied behavior plan as appropriate homeschooling.

Over the course of the year, the twins' immediate improvements were impressive: language skills, using utensils, potty training. We came to believe they would be ready to move from homeschooling to mainstream schooling for grade school the next fall.

We thought that being exposed to the socialization of mainstream schooling would be positive for them, so we began looking into elementary schools. The responses we received to Austin and Christian's needs were mostly unwelcoming. Many of the schools claimed not to have the necessary resources to deal with our boys' special requirements. We understood the problems with funding and resources—we even told several schools that we would pay for any costs to bring in aides. But I think the demands on the system were still fairly new and maybe the administrators were surprised by what was required to meet the needs of children with autism.

One of our therapists eventually recommended Trinity Lutheran Christian School, which was just thirty minutes away, in Portland. We introduced ourselves and our boys, and the principal of the school thought that having Austin and Christian enrolled would be a positive part of the learning experience for the neurotypical children.

The first thing we did was invite all the other parents to a meeting. We gave them packets filled with information about autism that we collected from doctors and therapists. We told them what to expect in terms of the boys' behavior. We never thought that autism was a free pass for our kids to misbehave. Some things were uncontrollable, but certain behaviors were unacceptable regardless of what health problems they had. We told parents and teachers that we expected the boys to be mannered and accountable. The teachers and schoolmates loved our boys and wanted to help, and the boys were inspired by the positive environment. It was such a good experience for all of us that we pulled Jonathan from his Camas public school after the third grade and enrolled him at Trinity until he graduated from eighth grade.

In first and second grade, Austin and Christian were behind in school because of their language skills, but they effectively interacted with the teachers and students and were doing so well—with appropriate behavior—that we began hosting playdates with other children at our home. By third grade, with the lessons growing more difficult, the boys fell further behind. Their behavior became so erratic and distracting that we had to withdraw them from school and resume homeschooling. Their being in the classrooms just wasn't fair to the other children.

In 2002, Christian began one of the most alarming behaviors we would see over the years: head banging. Austin did it occasionally as well, but not as often or as violently as his twin brother. Christian would lie down and begin pounding his head against the floor, or lean against a wall and bang his head there. We were told it was a symptom of his autism, but there were no explanations for why it suddenly surfaced when it did. It was shocking to see. One time he ended up in a trauma ward for a CT scan after banging his head so hard against a concrete wall that he bloodied himself.

Dr. Jennifer Reid, a naturopathic doctor from Gresham, Oregon, treated the twins from 2002 through 2007. She got Christian fitted with a helmet, but he simply learned to take it off and start banging again. Despite countless doctor visits and our repeated attempts to stop him or console him, Christian kept banging his head on the floor.

I know it seems logical to think that a parent could stop a child from doing such a thing. Right? If we couldn't reason with the twins or discipline them, we surely were bigger and stronger and could physically control them. Right? We certainly tried. We held Christian and cradled him and pulled him away from anything he could bang his head on, but he wouldn't stop. We might divert him for a short time, but the second he could get away from us, he'd start again. It also seemed that our attempts to intervene only increased his resolve. It wasn't a light tapping, either. It was done with force. It was something I would never get used to seeing.

We became aware of a medical theory about such self-harm that attempts to offer an explanation. It's been suggested that some children with autism engage in these kinds of behaviors so that the pain inflicted will distract them from other pain somewhere else in their bodies. Our doctors theorized that Christian's head banging could have something to do with pain he was experiencing in his stomach. The doctors also explained that self-injurious behaviors can act as a means of communication. When they break the rules, neurotypical children might talk back—or lie, or rationalize—or they may yell at their parents when they're angry or frustrated by something. Being largely unable to communicate, our twins didn't have those verbal outlets. So they might communicate their frustration and anger by hitting something, or hitting themselves, or biting themselves.

While Austin didn't bang his head as often as Christian, he started biting his hand when he was frustrated or mad about something. He wanted to take it out on something or somebody. He knew he couldn't strike out at us, so he'd punch or kick a hole in the wall, or he'd hit himself, sometimes in the face.

Based on our doctors' advice, we began focusing on trying to calm the twins' self-injurious behavior by controlling their diet and supplements more effectively. There was a great deal of trial and error involved. We saw positive results, especially with Christian, and it is one of the approaches that has paid consistent dividends over the years. We can't be sure what the exact trigger for his stomach pain was, but the effects of his medications seemed related. There was no permanent solution, however, and the head banging and other self-injurious behavior would return and sometimes intensify. The sight and sound of it was sickening, and the inability to comfort the twins or stop them felt like such a failure. We tried everything we could think of, and every time we couldn't stop them, our hearts would break a little more.

CURT

Ana led the way with her online research on ASD and with keeping up on the theories about treatments. She spent every day with the twins when I was at work, so she was keenly attuned to trends in their behavior. Being away from the house during most days, though, allowed me to shape some perspectives that were different from Ana's.

Austin was the dominant twin even before he and Christian were born, and it continued to be that way as they grew. They seemed like two halves of one person—completely opposite, but together they equaled a full personality. Austin was always the extrovert—to an extreme degree. He tried so hard to communicate that he got very loud and in your face. He's not somebody who would ever sneak up on you. Other than during his meltdowns, Christian was always so quiet and introverted. Maybe it's like this for many sets of twins, but this degree of polarity in their personalities is extremely pronounced with Austin and Christian. Even when they ate, they were the opposite. Give them a pizza, and Austin would eat the toppings and Christian would eat the crust. Maybe Christian would like the toppings, too, but Austin usually got them first and Christian ended up settling for the crust. We could try to manipulate any imbalances to even things out for Christian whenever possible, but they seemed pretty set in their roles and comfortable in being their half of the pair. They rarely had scuffles, but that's probably because Christian habitually deferred to Austin. For twins who have grown up so closely, they actually interacted pretty rarely. Because his health was always more of a concern than Austin's, Christian was far less active than his twin. He didn't try to communicate as much and often was withdrawn from his brothers.

Jonathan grew apart from the twins, too. He used to play all the time with his brothers, who were so close in age they were almost like triplets. Once they started showing symptoms, however, the twins stopped wanting to mix it up with him in physical play. They started pulling away from him, and you could sense that Jonathan was hurt by it. He could tell something had changed about the twins. Even when we got the diagnosis on the twins, we didn't know how to explain it to Jonathan. We tried to keep it simple, telling him that their brains worked a little differently. He seemed to understand that we needed to be patient and spend more time with them. If he didn't understand, he at least stopped asking for explanations.

It wasn't easy for him. At times when they were young, Austin and Christian would start biting each other. Jonathan would try to intervene, as a good big brother would, and sometimes they'd both end up biting him. But Jonathan understood the importance of his role as the older brother.

When he was in second or third grade, he asked his teacher if he could help with the kids in the special needs class. He said he wanted to because he knew how to make them smile. He explained to the teacher that he had learned how while dealing with his brothers.

Siblings get jealous in just about any family, but when others require a great deal more help, the resentment can grow. Jonathan, though, mostly kept his feelings to himself.

Curt's induction into the Seattle Seahawks Ring of Honor, 1994.

CHAPTER 8

OUR OWN PRIVATE ISLAND

ANA

Even at the point where their cognitive and communication skills stalled, the twins kept growing and getting stronger. Their enhanced physical abilities meant they were able to find new avenues for trouble through their preteen years. We worked hard at trying to anticipate the kinds of predicaments they might find themselves in, but we were hampered in our planning by adult logic. It took us a while to realize the twins simply weren't frightened by situations that should, naturally, lead to caution.

Because they didn't have fears, Curt and I had to have the fears for them.

I worried that they might see something dangerous that could intrigue them if they were ever on their own. Austin, the master escape artist, presented the greatest concerns. When he was about five, Austin sneaked out of the house when we had visitors. It happened so fast: people were coming in, and as we greeted them, Austin disappeared. We couldn't find him. We had everybody scatter around the house to see if he was hiding, and when we couldn't locate him, we organized ourselves into a search party and went through the neighborhood.

I had been taking the boys out walking regularly for exercise, so when Austin disappeared, I thought of the things that had interested him during those times when we made our way around the neighborhood. Austin was always fascinated by water—near the point of obsession, really. Neither of the twins knew how to swim, but they always wanted to get closer to water whenever they saw it. There was a golf course near our house, and I always tried to stay away from it on our walks because of the water-hazard ponds that I knew might tempt him if he got away.

Once, though, Austin saw another little pond in our neighborhood on one of our walks. As the rest of the family and visiting friends scoured the neighborhood and knocked on doors, I sprinted straight toward that pond. I tried to estimate how long he'd been gone and how far he could have gotten in that time. He easily had enough time to get to the pond. The worst-case scenarios raced through my mind as I ran. Not only could he have reached the pond, he could have gotten in, and . . . Thinking of the possibilities made me frantic.

As I neared the pond, I heard splashing. I yelled out, "Austin! Austin!" There he was. He had stripped down naked and was playing in shallow water. He was having a ball. The water wasn't very deep, but he was very near a big culvert pipe that ran down to a lake. It all could have easily been fatal with just one small slip. A few moments with the door open was all it took to put his life in danger.

CURT

Austin amazes us with his cleverness. That's not always a good thing for parents trying to keep their eyes on him.

He got very comfortable with computer technology at a young age. He probably wasn't ten yet when we took him off the computer for doing something he shouldn't have. Ana disconnected the computer and told him that it was broken. It didn't take Austin long before he had everything put back together and up and running.

Another time, Austin wasn't allowed to print anything off the computer because he'd gone through so much ink and paper. He would go through a ream of paper if you didn't watch. He wasn't happy that we had limited his access to the printer, so he decided to do something about it. The next morning at about dawn, he somehow slipped out of the house to run over to the home of our neighbors Don and Alison Lovell. Alison's father was there visiting and was already awake. The man had to have been surprised to see a young boy at the door at that early hour. Austin pointed at our house by way of introduction. Her father was comfortable enough with that explanation and let him in. Austin hurried off to the Lovells' computer room and was busy printing pages and pages until they got up an hour or more later. If his sneaking out of the house hadn't scared us so much, we would have admired his determination.

ANA

All of Austin's sneaking out caused us to become even more militant with our safeguards for the twins. I didn't like the idea of turning our house into a jail. No mother would feel comfortable with that idea. But we had to have better control over where the twins were at all times. If it felt restrictive to the kids, well, we were sorry, but safety was more important than anything else.

How far did we go in our efforts to fortify the compound? Curt had a six-foot-tall wooden fence built to encircle the yard. It was impressive—taller than me and absolutely impermeable. The day it was finished, Austin ran up to it and climbed over the top as if he were one of those "ninja warriors" going through obstacle courses on television. He was gone like it wasn't even there, like it was just another challenge. He was such an amazing climber, always testing himself. He could get up a tree in a matter of seconds. Then what? I certainly couldn't climb up and get him. Outside, inside, it didn't matter—Austin never stopped. One time he climbed to the top of an entertainment center and fell off before I could get to him. He was dazed, so we had to call 911 to have EMTs check him over. It wasn't that we weren't there watching. He was just so fast and athletic that he could be on top of something anytime you weren't within arm's reach of him.

Austin had been like that since he was very little. A therapist recommended aversion therapy and had us buy a bullhorn that we were supposed to use whenever we saw Austin climbing. We were expected to carry around the bullhorn all day and scream at him when he started his climb. The loud noise was supposed to scare him, even if he had no fear of falling from heights. It seemed impractical, but we gave it a try. The thunderous sounds didn't faze him a bit, didn't even slow him down. But it was a jolt to everybody else in the house, and practically everybody in the neighborhood was alerted to the fact that Austin was climbing on something in our house.

Christian was stealthier. One evening I got a call from a neighbor who was worried because she could see that Christian had somehow opened a window on the second floor and was pushing against the screen. She thought he was about to fall out the window. It was a real possibility, and with the second floor being fifteen feet or higher, it was a very dangerous possibility.

As much as we tried to anticipate dangers, the twins' most danger-ous actions were things that wouldn't cross our minds until they started doing them. We decided we had to go into lockdown mode.

We gradually stopped inviting friends to our house. The chance of emotional meltdowns any minute, or the possibility of one of the twins suddenly kicking holes in the wall, wasn't something we wanted our friends exposed to. More than that, we realized that having company could be a distraction for us, that the risk for something dangerous to happen increased when we didn't have our full attention on the boys—just as it did the day Austin got out on his own and ended up in the pond.

The dangers of their running off were obvious. On their own, Austin and Christian were unable to communicate who they were, where they lived, or what their health issues were. They wouldn't be conscious of the danger of oncoming vehicles if they got out on the street, nor would they be able to find their way home. The scenarios were terrifying, so we installed an elaborate locking and alarm system to keep the boys inside the house. A signal would go off whenever a door or window was opened, and an announcement would inform us of exactly which door or window it was.

I wear the master control for the locks and alarms on a lanyard around my neck. I'm never without it. It didn't seem right at first to be so militant about where they were from minute to minute. It didn't feel like it would be a great environment for kids, but then something would happen to remind us that we always had to be on guard.

I would take the lanyard with all the keys and alarms off when I went to sleep. I didn't want to end up choking myself by wearing it overnight, so I put it on my nightstand where it would be handy if I needed to get it at a moment's notice in the dark. Austin apparently noticed that I took it off for sleep. I woke up one night and saw that the lanyard was gone. I went downstairs, where I heard noises coming from the kitchen. We found him gorging himself on the food from the unlocked pantry. We were lucky he didn't use the keys to get out of the house or to get into things more hazardous than pastries. I had to start hiding the lanyard under the mattress when I slept.

Their wandering off when we were in public was one of our constant fears. The twins were so set on seeing *Disney on Ice* in Portland one year that I decided to bring a sitter to help so I wouldn't be outnumbered by them. The boys were very well behaved during the show, but when we got up to go, Christian somehow got caught up in the crowd and walked away. I thought the sitter had him; she thought I had him. This could happen to any child in a crowd. But the twins at that point were big enough to cover a lot of ground. And they didn't have the instinct to turn and look for us, or get cautious if they were approached by a stranger or neared traffic.

We shouted for a while before I saw him. He'd gone about sixty feet with the crowd, but was still in the building. My heart froze. It's the worst sick feeling you can have. I must have yelled louder then, because he finally heard me call his name and stopped.

Curt says he has had to learn how to sleep with one eye open. He's only partly kidding. They could take off and vanish in the time it takes to blink. The last time we went to Disneyland, I took the cushions off the couch in our hotel room and slept on the floor by the door so there was no way they could get out without waking me up.

The safest approach to life was just to spend most of the time at home, where locks and monitoring systems help shepherd the boys. That was why we didn't get out in the world. Staying home where we could control the environment and keep them safe just made a lot of sense to us. Maybe it kept the boys from being better socialized, but it was the choice we made.

This was our life, and it became a very real isolation.

CURT

People thought we had disappeared.

Friends and old teammates asked me why they didn't see us anymore, why I didn't take part in more of the Seahawks alumni festivities or golf outings, or make public appearances like so many of the other former players. Why wasn't I in a broadcast booth doing color commentary or something like that? I often tried to just dodge the question. I was busy. I had work. Lots to do. Sometimes they sounded kind of suspicious, like Ana and I had turned into recluses for some reason. In a way, we had. But it wasn't because we were trying to be antisocial. Ana needed me at home. The kids needed me home. I couldn't be obligated to anything that required me to travel and be on the road very often. That would leave Ana with around-the-clock responsibility for the kids. I had to be close to home in case something happened. And I wanted to have a job with some flexibility. There was no big mystery—it was just what we had to do. There wasn't any conscious effort on our parts to pull away from the public. We didn't withdraw from our life, this *was* our life.

At first, I didn't talk to people about it because I didn't understand the diagnosis enough to answer all the questions they were likely to have. Then, as things developed, I didn't want to talk about it because I didn't want people to feel sorry for us. I also thought that if I told anybody the reason, it might sound like I didn't think Ana was capable of handling the kids on her own. None of that was the case, of course, but you don't know how people will interpret things they don't understand.

Ana said that sometimes she felt like she was the jailer for the kids, but we were living inside the jail, too. Having twins with autism made it much harder for us to get babysitters. We couldn't ask some young neighbor kid to be responsible if the boys started kicking the walls or having meltdowns. Those were difficult situations even for us, as their parents, to deal with.

The few times I did have to take trips for business, I'd come back and Ana obviously would be worn down. Parenting in any case is a huge job, but Ana's role went beyond that. She is the CEO of the Warner family. When the boys were young, she wasn't just keeping her eyes on them, she was helping with therapies and treatments and organizing all the appointments and prescriptions, and cooking everything from scratch. She had to bathe them and clean them and clean up after them. Every day. Around the clock.

I got a true understanding of how much she did when Ana went back to Brazil to see her aging parents. The twins were midteens, and I was in charge—flying solo. It was brutal. I had to try to keep up with the dietary regimen they were on, something that on its own is a massive effort. It wasn't like we could just get some drive-through burgers. "Cheating" with processed foods might disrupt everything we had been working on with our efforts to ease some of the twins' stomach problems. Ana had worked double duty before she left, making all the meals ahead of time and leaving me with the instructions. She had it intricately plotted, which meals for which days, even giving me a list of the things I had to take out of the freezer ahead of time for the next day.

I took the time off work even though the twins were in school at the time and were gone part of the day. There was no way I would have made it through her time away without all the prep work she did. I knew she worked hard, but to have to jump in and do even a part of it myself gave me a real appreciation for what her days were like and how hard that job is. I was exhausted when she got home from that short trip. I had to marvel that she'd been doing all this day in and day out for years.

With such a workload, we simply didn't have time to think about our social lives. Over time, the only friends who still visited were our neighbors, the Lovells. They've remained close and kept their arms open to us, even after the day they invited our entire family to come for a dip in their new pool and Austin got in the water and pooped. We were mortified, of course, but the Lovells were very gracious. They understand what it means to be friends with our family and have us as guests to their home. Accidents happen, they said, no big deal. But Ana and I wanted to find a rock to crawl under.

Sometimes I drop my head into my hands and marvel that we made it through those years. I felt it was a father's duty to take care of the boys. It was my job to keep them safe. To keep my whole family safe. But I just couldn't help them through some things. They are my children and I love them, but nothing I tried really helped them. I had this sense of failure. I tried my best, but it wasn't anywhere close to good enough.

Maybe I can explain this best by sharing it through my eyes, by telling exactly what it feels like to watch your children bang their heads bloody. There is a frantic, desperate look in their eyes, there's fear and pain. It's like they're trying to say, *Help me, help me,* but you're helpless to stop them from banging their heads on something hard. And the sound is the stuff of nightmares. You don't know how long it will last or how bad it will get.

Doctors will tell you that they're trying to make themselves feel one kind of pain to overcome some different kind of pain. It makes you think, *How bad must that pain be that it makes banging their heads on the floor seem like a good option?*

Meltdowns are different. They put their hands over their ears or flap their hands, and they scream at a pitch you can't imagine. They seem so overwhelmed. I would try to hug them and comfort them, but sometimes that was exactly the opposite of what they needed. They didn't want to be touched. So nothing I could do was the right thing. I would look into their eyes, and it's like they were asking me, *Why? Why is this happening to me?* I wanted to say, *I don't know!*

To celebrate Thanksgiving in 2004, we accepted an invitation to the house of our friends, the Riveras. We knew any trip could come off the rails pretty quickly, so we had to be on high alert, and in this case we didn't even get into the Riveras' home. As we were getting out of the car, Christian crunched down so he could bang his head on the back seat floorboards. But instead of hitting the floorboard, he hit the metal rail anchoring the front seat and split his forehead wide open. Blood was gushing everywhere. We ended up spending that Thanksgiving in a hospital trauma center.

Another time, Austin decided to kick the window of his room. The glass shattered, and we found him with a big piece of glass sticking out of his leg—blood all over everything. I drove him to the hospital while Jonathan held on to his leg. He had more than thirty stitches—and never cried once. Didn't cry. He was just a young boy with this giant gash, but he apparently felt no pain or fear. It was amazing, and it was sickening.

Such chaos, we decided, was more manageable in one familiar space—our home. With all its locks and alarms, and the dangerous things hidden away, we had as much control as we could manage.

For a while, we had a motor home we would drive places as a family. It was a way for us to get away and still keep the environment mostly controlled. But we had to sell it so we could afford to remodel the house to fix all the holes that had been kicked into the walls, as well as reinforce everything to meet "Austin" standards.

If I ever took time to stop and focus on it, sure, there were a lot of things I would have liked to have done as a family that we couldn't do. But this was how we felt we needed to live our life. The house had become our own private island.

CHAPTER 9

ENDING IT . . .

2006–2007

ANA

Riding in the car calmed the twins. Maybe it was the motion, the steady vibration, or the sound of the spinning wheels. Whatever it was, the combination acted like a soothing lullaby for them. Almost nothing else quieted them for such a long time.

I would often take them for rides with no destination. I'd just drive out on the country roads to get away. It's really beautiful where we live in Washington. As I drove, the fir trees flashed past, the wheels hummed, and the boys were still. Those quiet moments had gotten so rare that I came to cherish them. I soon became very familiar with every one of the back roads around Camas. They were my refuge. I appreciated the car as one of the few things in my out-of-control life that I could steer in the direction that *I* wanted to go.

Curt and I worried that the amount of attention needed to manage the twins kept us from having special time with Jonathan. We agreed that we would try to balance things out for Jonathan by having Curt focus on nurturing the kind of bonding through sports that he had shared with his father. Baseball, soccer, basketball, football—the games changed with the seasons; the most important part was the time they shared. We knew Jonathan had to feel shortchanged by our attention to the twins, so we were trying to make his life as normal as possible with Curt's close involvement.

This approach meant that I would spend most of my time with the twins, so when they became uncontrollably active, or I felt they might be on the verge of a meltdown, I would take them for a drive. I was lucky—Curt still had his car dealership, which meant I had access to demo cars that were available for test drives or use by the staff. Every five thousand miles I would have to change cars, and I went through those miles! I would go through five thousand miles in two or three months, just driving the twins around the back roads.

During those hours in the car, without the almost-constant disruption that was common in the house, I was able to think. The twins would be sitting quietly in the back seat, distracted by the constantly changing scenery or the movement of the car over the hills and around corners. It felt a little like meditation—for all of us, I suppose. The more time I had to think and reflect about my life, the darker my thoughts grew. The boys' behaviors were so intense; the screaming and kicking and biting went on almost around the clock. I was just so tired, and there was no indication that our lives were going to get any less complicated. They might even get worse!

I had been diagnosed with postpartum depression and later PTSD. Depression can be a hard thing to recognize in yourself. It was difficult for me to realize how much of a hold depression had on me. I wouldn't admit it to myself, let alone anybody else at the time. At the root of it, I still considered myself to blame for just about every problem we had. I believed that as the mother of the family, I was supposed to make everything right, and as the twins neared twelve, our family certainly wasn't close to being right in my eyes. It wasn't for a lack of trying. In fact, part of what was so demoralizing was that I was making everybody else miserable by "over" trying, by pushing too hard. I had become obsessed, making rigid schedules, being strict about the diets, and clashing constantly with Curt or "Grandma" Hutcherson. Anybody under the Warner roof needed to go along with my plan or they would hear criticism. I was determined to see these boys recovered, or healed, or whatever I was supposed to call it—and I would do it by myself if I had to.

I was still clinging to some concept of what I thought a "normal" life would be. I wanted to be able to go out like a regular family and enjoy normal things . . . movies, games, parks. I started resenting everything. In the process of trying to heal the children, I had become some other person—a person I didn't like very much. The only change I could see happening was that everything was getting harder and seemingly more hopeless. Without regular sleep, without progress by the boys, my frustration mounted. It kept coming back to my struggle with being out of control.

I didn't want to live anymore. Living was too hard. Living overwhelmed me. For months I thought about ending it all. Many times in that car, with the twins, I considered driving off the road. Into a tree. Anything. Just something that would put an end to the constant struggle.

It truly wasn't about ending my pain. I didn't think I was being selfish, although it sounds like it now. I had this feeling that I would be doing Curt and Jonathan a favor. I thought it would be better for them if they didn't have the burden of me and the twins. I thought about it a lot, especially on those drives. I'd be in tears while I was driving, crying so hard I could barely see.

I had done this tearful drive with the twins on the back roads around Camas more times than I could count. So often I was overcome with emotion and depression. One day, on one of my drives with the twins, I found a radio station, K-Love. It was a Christian station. The music played, the miles passed, and I made it to the next day. The songs just ministered to me.

I used to call the station to ask for prayers so often that once when I missed a few days, someone at the station called me to check if I was all right. I was at home when they reached me; the kids were screaming and in such a state that I had to hang up. That made the people at the station afraid for me. Surely they sensed how vulnerable I was. They called again the following night to check on me.

I don't know how long it took, but gradually over time the music helped me think more positively. I was reminded of my core beliefs, of why I was here, and how important I was to my family. I believe in God, and didn't want to have to stand in front of Him and explain why I had done something horrible to myself and to our children—to His children. That's what made the difference for me. As bleak as it got, it was my faith and my love for God that kept me from doing that really stupid thing.

I never spoke to Curt about how deeply depressed I'd gotten. I worried that if I told him, the pressure would just be too much for him at a time when he already had so much to shoulder. He was holding up his end of our agreement with Jonathan and running his business and helping me with the twins. It wouldn't be fair to make my depression something else he had to worry about.

We needed to be together. This life was hard for everybody in the family, and they all needed me. I'm so grateful that I found a way up out of the deepest pit of desperation. I think, now, of everything I would have missed, and how much the family would have suffered, and how senseless a thing it would have been.

CURT

I knew Ana was hurting, but she did a good job of putting a mask on her emotions.

She had been diagnosed with PTSD, and I knew that could be serious, but like any mom, she didn't make taking care of herself a priority. The boys always came first. She demanded so much of herself, making every meal by hand, planning the diets and the supplements, researching every new possible treatment, and tending to the twins' every need. She's a perfectionist, and I think the pressure to sustain her high expectations was showing in her short temper and constant anxiety. I was worried about her, of course, but I trusted her when she told me she was okay. I didn't want to grill her or put more stress on her to tell me what was going through her mind.

For so much of the twins' youth, we were both in a dark, dark place, in a deep hole. I always thought at some point we would see a light at the end of the tunnel. We just had no idea how long the tunnel was. Maybe it would get even darker. That realization can take a person down, way down.

I wish I had known then how deeply she had been hurting. Depression can be a life-and-death condition, but I didn't know enough about depression at the time to spot it. Ana thought she was protecting me by not telling me about the thoughts she was having. She was acting on the same motives I felt when I thought I was protecting her by keeping silent with my frustrations in the early days after the twins' diagnosis. In reality, talking to each other honestly in both cases would have been the best thing for us all.

CHAPTER 10

PUBERTY WAS A NIGHTMARE

2004–2007

ANA

By their early teens, the boys were still receiving therapy and an array of treatments, but new and changing symptoms kept us from closing in on anything that worked for very long. Austin started licking windows. He'd steal dog food from the bowl of our Labrador, Lucky. He'd eat popcorn off the movie theater floor and the gum that he would find under tables. We were watching him constantly, but he got so quick at spotting something and putting it in his mouth that we sometimes couldn't stop him. He became an indiscriminate eating machine.

We were feeding him healthy food and appropriate portions at meals, but he would act like he was starving. Doctors told us there was a possibility that he couldn't sense when he was full, so his brain wouldn't tell him it was time to stop eating. That's why the pantry had to be locked. He would go in there and eat until it was empty.

Christian, on the other hand, would barely eat, except for strange nonedible things, like string. Or he would unravel thread from his socks and eat that. Our doctors told us the strange eating habits were related to fungal infections, or candida, in the boys' guts. It became a problem for Christian, affecting his health and creating great discomfort for years—perhaps causing the continued head banging and other self-injurious behavior. But so many other activities went unexplained. Austin would sometimes urinate on the floor in the house. Sometimes on a wall. Sometimes on our computer. Sometimes he would even pee on his brother. We asked their doctors what would cause him to do that, but there were no answers, no specific stimulus to logically attach the behavior to. It was just another mystery. A very unpleasant mystery.

Both twins engaged in unusual repetitive movements, known as self-stimulation, or "stimming." The theory is that when the world seems unpredictable and outside their control, some on the autism spectrum will wave their hands or repeat certain behaviors so they can focus their attention on that rather than on the outside stimulus that's bothering them. To those unfamiliar with the disorder, the movements seem inexplicably odd. Christian did more stimming than Austin. He would flap his hands and then cover his ears as he screamed, and at times, instead of screaming, he'd groan or growl. If something made him happy, he'd start bouncing and jumping in place. Austin tended to be more violent in his reactions to things that made him uncomfortable or frustrated—for example, he would kick holes in the walls.

Puberty was a nightmare. Adding hormones into the mix caused the twins' behaviors to become more destructive. And with their increasing physical strength, the boys seemed on the verge of demolishing the house. There were holes in the walls everywhere.

So we tried harder, giving a shot to almost anything that might help.

Sensory dysfunction can be a problem for some children with autism, as they can become hypersensitive to touch and to certain textures, sometimes to the point of pain. At times the boys' skin could be so sensitive they would tear apart their garments just trying to be rid of the bothersome feeling of the tags. I learned to snip the tags off before the boys would wear their clothes.

We tried a series of treatments geared to reducing the sensory dysfunction. We read about a certain apparatus that could comfort them— it was a hammock-like swing that we bolted to the ceiling in one of the bedrooms. It was made of a strong Lycra fabric, and when they would lie inside it, the fabric would cling to the boys like a cocoon. It provided a comforting pressure on their bodies. They loved it. We would rock them, and we used it as positive reinforcement. But it only soothed them when they were actually in it.

There were other messier options that were suggested. One was a pit filled with plastic balls, similar to what you might see in some of the chain hamburger places. Another was a large gym mat that we covered with shaving cream for the boys to slide around in as a means of reducing their sensitivity issues. We also tried filling a large tub with uncooked rice in which the boys would sit. Seriously, there was a time when we had a huge barrel of rice in our house. They liked it, but they got bored with it after a while, and, of course, rice was everywhere. They liked these treatments and had fun, but ultimately there were no lasting health or behavioral effects to come from any of them—and they all were nightmares to clean.

On someone else's advice for dealing with the boys' sensitivities, we would brush the twins' arms and legs. They loved the attention, and we felt better for having given it a try. If it did nothing but allow them to feel a closeness with us, to sense how much we cared about them, it was worth the effort. These experiences reminded us, again, of how lucky we were to have the time and resources to try such things.

The constant strain and effort to come up with solutions to the twins' changing symptoms ate away at us, though. We could cope with the repairs to the house and inconveniences, the extra effort and the expenses, but seeing the twins in pain was heartbreaking. High among our fears was the nagging notion that someday they'd outsmart us and a truly hazardous situation would present itself.

It seemed the stakes were raised one day when Austin sneaked behind me in the kitchen and got a carving knife off the counter. I was right there, but by the time I saw him, he was stabbing the couch. He later told me that he saw the couch as the dragon in the movie *Sleeping Beauty*, and he was Prince Phillip, using his sword to kill the dragon. In the moment, it didn't seem like he was just acting out a scene. I could see in his eyes how serious he was. I knew I had to be very calm and approach him slowly.

"Okay, Austin, that's enough." I almost whispered it, trying not to alarm or provoke him. "Put the knife down now, Austin."

Damage to the couch was a small concern next to the very real danger of what could have happened if he had directed his fantasy toward something other than a piece of furniture. At times when the twins were angry at my having to take things away from them or discipline them, they'd call me the name of some evil woman in a Disney movie: Cruella De Vil or Maleficent. I remembered that Maleficent had turned herself into the dragon that Prince Phillip killed with his sword in *Sleeping Beauty*. I knew Austin would never try to hurt me. But such serious role-playing was something Curt and I realized we had to watch more closely. We were concerned that he was increasingly mixing fantasy with reality.

Toward the end of 2007, I made a list of things I needed to remind myself of, hoping to appreciate certain things that might get lost in the daily craziness, and to realize that some things were just a part of my life that I had to accept. My twins couldn't always communicate love for me, but I still knew they loved me. I realized that my kids didn't know the things in their lives that they should fear for their own well-being. So I had to fear all those things for them.

My entry halfway down that list addressed a worry that simmered in my mind after we had to put so many locks on the windows and doors. It read: *No. 5—Pray that the Lord protects us from fire.*

CURT

At times I'd get flashbacks to football games when things were going bad. Sometimes you're getting beaten and there's nothing you can do about it. No matter what you do—the game plan, substitutions, trick plays—you're still just getting a beatdown. What do you do? You have no choice, you've got to line up and try it again. The next play, boom, you get clobbered again. Play after play. The only thing you can do is just keep going back at it and keep trying to do your best. Sometimes you just have days like that. That's pretty much what every day felt like for us for a long time.

We decided that one thing we could do, in the fall of 2007, was to start a major renovation of the house to reinforce and strengthen all the lower walls with heavy wainscoting. We figured if the walls were so strong they wouldn't break, then the twins might stop kicking. We knew, of course, that they might just move on to something else, but it was worth a try.

The construction team came out with some of the material to test before we started ordering wood and getting the project going. The guys held up the sheet of wood, and we gave Austin the green light to go ahead and give it his best shot. He turned his back so he could kick it like a mule. He broke through the wood like a martial arts expert. The workers were stunned. It was decided we needed stronger wood.

It was a huge project, but it seemed a wise investment in protecting the house. When it was finished in late 2007, the house looked beautiful—like new—and every wall was undamaged.

Sadly, it didn't last long.

Curt with Isabella.

CHAPTER 11

SHE'S ONE
TOUGH COOKIE

Fall 2007

ANA

The twins were twelve when we adopted Isabella. Our house was filled with some degree of chaos most of the time, so adding another little human to this might have been considered questionable by some—including my husband, Curt.

Maybe so, but adopting a child was something that I'd wanted to do since I was very young, growing up in Brazil. I was a teenager when somebody in my neighborhood was gathering donations of clothes and shoes for an orphanage. I helped them make the collections and went to the orphanage to help with the delivery. It broke my heart to see all those little kids who were there and had nothing. Nothing. No shoes, just the ragged clothes on their bodies. There was such severe poverty. I felt awful for those children—there were so many of them. That was something I never forgot, like a lingering obligation.

My perfect plan was to have two kids and then adopt after that. But we lost Ryan, and then all of a sudden, we had three sons. It seemed like there would never be a right time to add another child to the family. The house was full and things were hectic, granted, but I started thinking that if we didn't do it soon, we likely wouldn't get the chance. Curt and I would be getting too old for another young child. To me, it felt like the right thing.

I'm sure at the time I thought that adopting a baby might add some hope and normalcy to our lives. We really missed out on much of Jonathan's childhood because we spent so much time with the twins. And the experience with Austin and Christian was obviously extraordinary. I thought we needed a different parenting experience. We had three boys, so I felt a little girl would bring some sunshine into our house.

Curt was fine with adoption in theory. Strictly speaking, he had been adopted by his grandparents. But from his perspective, the timing wasn't optimal. He had reservations for the obvious reasons: two of our three sons were taking up a great deal of our focus, and we were in the middle of getting updates and repairs done to the house. Curt was right—it didn't make a lot of sense when you weighed those things. I could tell he wasn't exactly "all in" with the idea, but he went along with it, tentatively, for my sake.

I looked into adopting from Brazil first, still carrying those memories of the poor orphans I saw when I was young. But the paperwork was so complicated, it appeared that we had very little chance of getting one. They seemed intent on making it difficult. We then looked into an adoption agency that Pastor Hutch had started in the Seattle area. The process took a while, as it does, but eventually we were informed there was an eighteen-month-old girl who was currently in foster care and in need of a home. I drove up to Tacoma to meet her. When she came into the room, she was the little ray of sunshine I'd hoped for. She came right over to me, sat on my lap, and started talking to me. Her smile went straight to my heart. It was instant love.

The following week, I brought Curt and Jonathan up to meet her. As she had done with me, she went right over to Curt and lifted her little arms to him so he'd pick her up. It was beautiful. She stayed in his arms the whole time. Curt was defenseless. You could just see him melt as he got to know her.

She soon joined our family, with her adoption finalized in August 2008. We named her Isabella, and she's been such a gift. She carries pure joy and gives it to everyone she meets.

Isabella conducts her own special form of therapy with her older twin brothers. It's not complicated: she just loves them. She hugs them and gets them to interact with her. She gets them out of their shells a little bit. They join her in her little pretend tea parties. She's been a blessing. She even brings out a real tender side in Christian. Every morning when I wake her up, Christian will go in, sit on her bed, and give her a hug and a kiss good morning. If somebody is dancing on TV, Bella will call Christian and he'll go in and try to imitate the dancing with her. They're a real pair.

She likes to compete with Austin, both having such competitive spirits. Austin is always racing with her. Curt says that it's almost as if Austin and Bella are the twins, because their personalities are very similar.

We had the same worries about Isabella that we had with Jonathan, that she would get shortchanged because of our need to focus on caring for the twins. It was hard sometimes when she'd ask if we could go to the mall, and I had to tell her we couldn't because I didn't have anybody to watch the boys. It was hard to get a lot of time alone with her. But the twins became easier for us to care for in certain ways as they matured, taking less of our time and focus. By the time Isabella reached seven or eight, she had advanced beyond Austin and Christian in mental and cognitive development. So, in some ways, Isabella acts like she's the big sister, and because she's grown up in a family with three older brothers, she's one tough, tough cookie.

Isabella had seen her big brother Jonathan go off to college, and she asked me if Austin and Christian would do the same. I told her, "No, not unless there's a miracle and they get completely better, they probably won't be going to college."

Isabella replied, "That's okay, because I like them the way they are."

CURT

I wasn't opposed to the idea of adoption—in general. But for us? We had so much going on. The house was getting torn up. We were trying to get repairs and updates done. The twins were going through puberty and reaching new low points. I just thought our lives were too compli-cated. I didn't think it would be fair to bring a new child into the mix. But I went along with it for Ana. I knew that it was very important to her. It was a vision she had had for us for years, since we first discussed starting a family, so I let her drag me along through the early stages of the process.

Behind my tentative agreement to go along with it, I was hoping it wouldn't happen. I thought, *We're getting older, and now we will have to start over again?* I didn't like the sound of it. I didn't see Ana's logic.

I hoped it would be one of those times when you agree to some-thing that might not happen, all the while hoping you'll get credit from your wife for having been a good sport when it ultimately falls apart. But once I met Bella, I was fully on board. She was immediately part of the family from the start. There was no period of adjustment or any time when it was uncomfortable. She was a full-fledged part of the family from the first day; there were no more doubts or reservations.

We have a lot of fun, and she is terrific with the boys. She's a good athlete, too, very competitive. She kind of bosses Austin around a little bit. He can use that; he probably listens to her more than he listens to us. I asked her why she isn't as bossy with Christian, and she told me that Austin bosses him around enough, so Christian doesn't need more of it from her. Pretty insightful. She really does complete our family.

CHAPTER 12

THE HOUSE IS ON FIRE

February 2008

ANA

Trying to make our daughter Isabella's second birthday festive, Curt lit two little candles and then went back into the garage to hide the lighter. By that time we were well aware that sharp things and fire starters had to be locked up or hidden from Austin and Christian.

The twins were thirteen, with the strength and physical capabilities of other children their age. But their autism left them with the cognitive abilities of the typical four- or five-year-old. The combination of physical strength with the absence of judgment and understanding of dangerous consequences was a recipe for disaster.

A few days after the party, Jonathan woke up sick and decided to stay home from school. With him home, too, I sensed it was going to be a difficult day. Because I spent every day at home with the twins while Curt was running the car dealership, I developed a sixth sense for impending trouble. Call it a mother's intuition. It was especially true with Austin—always the wanderer, the unpredictable mischief-maker, the one who had such surprising problem-solving skills.

I told Curt my concerns that morning, and we discussed whether Curt should stay home, but he had an important meeting scheduled. It was his dealership, after all, so it was going to be hard to postpone a meeting just because his wife had a premonition. He kissed us all good-bye and told me to call if anything came up, or even if I just wore out and needed a break. He would be only fifteen minutes away and would drop everything if I needed help—meeting or no meeting.

By the afternoon, the kids were scattered throughout the house—and uncharacteristically quiet. We didn't have to keep an eye on the twins absolutely every minute anymore. I always had to check on them, of course, but there were enough times by this age that they could play quietly by themselves in their room without the constant monitoring.

At about two, I was braiding Bella's hair into pigtails in the family room. Christian had come down to watch *Sesame Street* with Isabella and me, and Jonathan was trying to fight off a bad case of bronchitis by dozing and relaxing in front of the television upstairs in the master bedroom. Christian didn't usually sit down with us for TV, but this day he did, leaving Austin alone in their room. I wanted everybody to keep quiet that afternoon so Jonathan could rest up and get better, and since Austin wasn't banging around in the twins' room, it seemed like everyone was on their best behavior.

Suddenly, the cry of the smoke alarm filled the house. I jumped. My adrenaline kicked in, and I was at a full run toward the stairs. The howling alarm could only mean one thing: fire.

As I approached the staircase, I saw Austin running from the kitchen and hurrying up the stairs carrying a small glass of water, his face a mask of guilt. The water instantly validated the fire alarm. He was trying to deal with a fire himself, hoping I wouldn't find out.

By the time I reached his room, the fire had already spread from the trash can to the curtains. Knowing that anything could happen in our house, and always trying to prepare for the worst, we made certain we had extinguishers ready and easily available. We didn't keep one in the twins' room, though, because we were sure they'd try to get into it to see how it worked. The closest extinguisher was in our master bedroom. I grabbed the extinguisher and ran back to the boys' room. I pulled the pin and aimed it at the flames that were now climbing up the wall. I squeezed the lever.

Nothing happened. It didn't work. The smoke thickened and turned black as it collected at the ceiling. The flames already had gone too far for me to be able to run and find another extinguisher. The kids had scattered downstairs.

"Jonathan," I screamed, "get the kids into the car!"

Already light-headed from the smoke inhalation, I ran down the stairs to get clean air and call 911. Once I knew the fire department was on its way, I called Curt.

"Curt . . . the house is on fire . . . we're getting out." I had already breathed in enough smoke to make talking difficult and painful, and there was no time to give him more details. I took a hurried mental inventory of the family. If Jonathan had the kids in the car, all I'd have to do would be pull it out of the garage, and we'd all be safe. Then I remembered our dog, Lucky, who'd been scared into hiding by the alarm.

The seconds ticked by. "Lucky! Lucky!" I called. He came, and I let him out in the backyard. What next? I opened the front door and turned off all the automatic locks and alarms so the firefighters could have quick access. Feeling faint now, I'd done all I could; I just needed to get to the garage and drive the car out. We'd all be fine.

"Mom . . . Mom!" Jonathan screamed from the mudroom. "I can't find Austin."

Oh, dear God, no! I almost collapsed under the weight of fearful possibilities. Austin was always a wild card; he might have gone anywhere. Curt and I made it an exercise at times to try to put ourselves in his mind. What would he try next? We always worried it might be the exact wrong thing. Knowing Austin, he might try to go back up to his room again to see if he could put out the fire, or maybe to save something important to him. I looked up the stairs from the family room, and the smoke, blacker now, was pushing its way down the stairs. The popping and sizzling was so loud it almost drowned out the shrieking alarm.

"Austin! . . . Austin!" I called, coughing between screams. No answer. I'd have to go up and get him. I pulled my shirt up to cover my nose and mouth, and started climbing the stairs. I stumbled and then just stayed low, inching forward, trying to get beneath the smoke.

Then I heard Jonathan shout up the stairs. "Mom, Mom, I found him . . . I've got him now . . . I've got Austin . . . let's go!" I gasped at the sound of Jonathan's news. I couldn't have gone much farther. I felt my way back down the stairs and out to the garage. I immediately did a head count. All accounted for, and all were safe. How Jonathan accomplished it, I'll never know, but it was heroic.

I eased the car out of the garage, but we were barely onto the driveway when an explosion shook the car like a bomb blast. Glass from the windows of the twins' room sprayed outward above us, shards scattering and reflecting the fire inside. Smoke from the upper floor rolled from the window, and flames curled back upward to engulf the roof.

In the back seat, Austin started laughing—laughing—just as he did during movies when scenes were colorful and loud. Jonathan shook him, hard, to get him to stop. Austin wasn't being mean or cruel, he just didn't understand, or maybe that was the only way he could express his intense feelings at the moment. Trying to regain my composure, I continued to back the car down the driveway. We were clear of the house, safe, but I couldn't take my eyes off the fire roaring out of the windows . . . until I backed into the streetlight with enough force to knock the pole to the ground and jar us all inside the car.

We were shaken, and now jolted by the collision, but unhurt. Moments later the firefighters arrived, and everything became a blur. Some hustled up onto the roof, chopping openings to vent the fire, others checked us over for injuries. They saw that I was struggling to breathe and gave me oxygen. It was hard to breathe it in without coughing. I couldn't stop shaking. I was dizzy—I felt ready to pass out.

Then I saw Curt. He was running down the road past the firefighters to get to us. I ripped off the oxygen mask and ran toward him the best I could. The look on his face was something I'd only seen once, that day in the hospital with Ryan. There was such fear in his eyes.

I kept nodding my head as I ran, trying to answer the question I knew was going through his mind. *Yes, we're all okay! Everybody is safe. We all got out.* When he understood the message, he slowed, stopped, and collapsed to his knees. Short of breath and wheezing when I got to him, I bent and cradled his head and whispered, "We're all okay . . . thank God . . . we're okay." We trembled as we hugged.

The firefighters who arrived at the scene were so brave and efficient, so quick to go about their dangerous job. They were inspiring in their efforts, and we are forever grateful to them and the others who do what they do.

It's a powerful thing to watch your home burn down. It was obvious as we looked at the house that so little—if anything—would be saved. My mind went through all the things that were inside: family treasures, pictures, things that couldn't be replaced. The fire gutted the inside of the house even though most of the exterior walls still stood. It's an image that still haunts me, but the feeling that always comes first when I think about that day is relief that no one was injured.

Even before the flames died out, I was worried about where we would stay, where we would live until we could find a new home. With our family, especially the twins, it would be hard to find a place that would be willing to open its doors to us. Of course we'd have to tell them ahead of time what the dangers might be. Fortunately for us, our neighbors rallied to our side and started making plans to help us.

Alison Lovell, our neighbor, invited us to stay at their house for however long it took to find a place to live. It was an immediate example of one of the best elements of human nature that we've found to be true: often, it is in the worst of times that you see the best in people.

So, the Lovells took us in. But we still had to figure out how to conduct the rituals and chores that filled our daily lives. Even if we were at someone else's house, we would have to keep a consistent environment and routine for the twins to avoid chaos and meltdowns. It was complicated and involved private moments we never told anybody about. The twins were thirteen, but I still had to be there to wash them in the shower and help with some basic hygiene—the duties of a mother with almost full-grown sons who weren't able to effectively clean themselves.

When I helped Austin in the shower that first night at the Lovells', I was still coughing and having trouble breathing. As I struggled to get him washed up, Austin broke down crying. He had just realized it was all real and his whole family could have been lost. We didn't often see strong emotions from the twins and, to that point, they hadn't developed a real understanding of the concepts of death and danger.

"Mama almost died," he said. His sweet innocence was so touching that I cried, too. He didn't want anybody to be hurt. It took the sight of me, covered in ash and coughing, for him to understand what had happened that afternoon, and he was so sorry about it that it broke my heart.

He explained that while he was in his room that afternoon, he thought he was Pinocchio inside the whale, Monstro, and the only way to get out was to light a fire, just as Pinocchio had. In his mind, it was all acting out a Disney movie.

When we looked back at the events that had to fall into place for that fire to get started, it seemed like Austin really had to plan it out. How did he get the lighter? Did he wait for Curt to go to work before getting it? Had he been fascinated by the way it lit the candles for Bella's birthday cake? Did he wait for me to be downstairs with Bella and Christian?

It seemed too complex for him to have planned in detail, even though he has an impressive ability to solve problems when he gets focused on something. We'll never know his thought process, but I completely believe him when he said he was trying to act out a scene in a Disney movie, and I know he had no idea he might burn the house down.

The fire chief asked questions, of course, and seemed to think I was just covering up for Austin. For legal purposes, he said, he had to consider filing charges of arson even though Austin was only thirteen. I told him what Austin had told me in the shower. He asked me, "Wait, your sons are thirteen and you still have to wash them?" When I explained why, he better understood the boys' stage of development and awareness. No charges would be filed, he said; it was an accident.

When we got all of the kids calm and to bed, I showered for a long time, but even with soaping and scrubbing, I couldn't wash the smell of our burning house off my hair and skin. When I closed my eyes, the image of the flames shooting out the windows was still there, like a photographic negative on the inside of my eyelids.

That night Curt tended to insurance reports and plans for the immediate future—including where our displaced family with special needs was going to live. When he finally came to the bedroom, I was still wet from the shower, and wearing a borrowed T-shirt. I was wheezing, and my eyes were red from the smoke and from crying. He hugged me and we prayed and gave thanks for the most important thing—the lives of our family.

CURT

It never mattered what kind of business I was in at the moment; when a call came from Ana, I took it. If she needed me at home, I'd be there. I knew she faced a dozen little dramas every day, and I wanted her to share anything she needed to with a phone call. I looked forward to her calls. Her voice has always been very distinctive. I loved it from the start, and even after all these years, a bit of her Brazilian accent lingered.

When the phone rang on the day of the fire, I could barely make out what she was saying. Her panic was obvious, especially with the fire alarm going off in the background. "The house is on fire, we're getting out." Click. That was all she said before hanging up.

Wait? What? I redialed and got no answer. I had to try to go back in my mind to piece together what she said. It was so sudden and out of context, I wasn't even sure I'd heard what she said. *Did she say the house is on fire? That can't be happening. Can it?* Was it even her or some kind of prank? I ran to the car and kept trying to call her back from my cell phone. It sounded as if she said they were getting out, but she didn't say they *were* out. My stomach kept churning as I drove home.

I had no idea of the time as I drove, nor how fast I was going. So many things were flashing through my mind, and everything in my experience told me that our house probably was not on fire. That just doesn't happen. As I got closer, I tried focusing on the sky in the direction of our house. I couldn't see smoke. Surely a house fire would put out a lot of smoke. Maybe it was something small. Maybe in the kitchen or the backyard. Maybe a false alarm . . . we had so many alarms at that point. Or maybe they had put it out already and everybody was safe.

Then I heard the unmistakable sounds of fire truck sirens. It all became real when I heard those fire trucks. This wasn't just some misunderstanding or false alarm or something getting too hot on the stove. Coming down the hill and around a corner, I finally saw the flames. The street was blocked. I jammed the car into park and started running past fire barricades that had been set up.

I could already see that the house was going to be lost, and I could see our car out in the street. Ana had to have driven it out, but where was everyone? I ran as hard as I could. Then, behind the car, I saw firefighters giving Ana oxygen. I knew then that the kids had to be safe or she wouldn't be there, outside getting oxygen—she'd be in the house trying to save them no matter what. I knew that for certain. She would not leave the house while anyone was still inside.

I don't know if she had been watching for me, but she saw me coming down the street and started running toward me. It seemed like the moment was in slow motion.

Ana was having trouble breathing and obviously was shaken up, but when she reassured me everyone was all right, I believed her, and I wept. After all she had gone through, she was the one calming me.

As the flames died down, I started thinking of all the practical things we'd have to take care of. With my worst fears set aside, I actually had a good thought: we had just remodeled the entire home to fix the damage done by the twins. After the remodel, a friend suggested I update my insurance policy to a level of coverage that reflected the increased value of the house. That turned out to be some very timely advice.

For a long time, it had felt as if we were living on the edge of something happening that was truly dangerous. We knew how unpredictable our lives were, and things could change without warning. Ana always had a deep fear of fire and worried about the gas lines. We knew, after Austin's duel with the couch, that knives had to be locked away. What else might Austin decide to reenact? But setting a fire to escape the belly of the whale? We didn't see that one coming. We thought we'd been careful with matches and the lighter, but it wasn't enough. And that cost us dearly.

Still, I knew we couldn't blame Austin. He didn't know what he was doing. We were very upset with him, but you couldn't really call it *angry*. Austin didn't start the fire to hurt anybody. He had no idea of the consequences.

The fire department let us back into the house that evening to see what was left. Mostly just the exterior walls stood, and some of the ground floor remained. The firefighters used the skylight to pump water into the house, so everything that wasn't burned was covered in sopping ash. We finished up that awful day the way we did so many other days. We hugged and we prayed. There wasn't any point in looking back, but of course we would for a long time. That night, we cried together. That's something you can always do. That's one of the things we learned: you never run out of tears.

CHAPTER 13

WHEN THE SMOKE CLEARED

CURT

The fire felt like a culmination of all the issues we'd been dealing with. The fire capped everything. This felt like we'd hit bottom. Or maybe this was below the bottom, worse than anything we could have pictured. What could be next? We'd been scrambling and working, trying to solve our problems. But this hit us hard. You know what, though? We lived through it. We pretty much lost everything. I had the clothes on my back. That was about it. But everybody was safe. It was time to start over.

When we got back in the house, we found that just about everything we had that wasn't burned was ruined by smoke or water damage, including the memorabilia I had left from my playing days. I was never one to build a monument to myself. Yes, I was proud to know there was a time when I was good at what I did, but I didn't need trophies to remind me. Football had been over twenty years before the fire. I had a wife and kids and a business. You can't stay stuck in the past. I was much more worried about my family. We had lost our home, so my personal things were insignificant. Memories of the years I'd played were good enough.

We didn't have time to sit there and complain and moan. We had to regroup and get focused. *What now? What do we do next?* I knew it would take a very long time to rebuild the house—if that was even a possibility. I imagined us trying to stay in a cheap hotel, but the twins could destroy a hotel room in a day or two. Plus, we couldn't all fit in one room, and if we had to get two, we'd have to have at least one of the adults staying in a room with the twins every night. It would mean physically splitting up the family, which was the opposite of what we needed at that time. It started to seem like we were facing a nearly impossible situation.

I called my accountant, Randy Taylor, in Bethesda, Maryland, to let him know what had happened and to get his advice about what we should do next. Randy then called another mutual friend, Scott Merrill, a stockbroker in Arizona. From there, Scott called a friend of his, Tony Glavin, a builder who actually lived very near us in Camas.

By a huge coincidence, Tony had just finished building a model home in a nearby development. I had never met Tony Glavin. I had no idea who he was, but this total stranger came to see us and offered us a home to live in. Through contacts with a series of friends, and Tony's good-heartedness, we moved into a brand-new model home just two days after the fire.

It was as quick as that—a series of three phone calls among friends, over a matter of minutes, and I went from desperation at our ill fortune to amazement at this blessing. All this was determined while our house was still smoldering.

Tony built that house as a model home to help promote the development, not for somebody to move into and live in. He especially didn't anticipate a potentially destructive family moving in the second it was finished. But he nonetheless arranged everything for us. The generosity stunned us. This felt like a rare case when our prayers were answered before we even had time to say them. *Amen!* Our considerate neighbors brought clothes and towels and bedding, and prepared dinners. They connected a television and put together a little bed for Isabella.

I have no way of knowing whether my having been a pro football player had anything to do with people's consideration and generosity. Maybe they had been Seahawks fans. I'd like to think that it's in people's nature to help others having a hard time. Here's what I *do* know: those dear friends really stepped up when we needed it the most. The sadness of that day has really never gone away, but the sense of generosity in the human spirit we experienced during that time is something we've never forgotten, either.

ANA

I began to have serious panic attacks. My chest would tighten so I could hardly breathe. My heart would pound so hard, and I'd have this overwhelming sense that I was going to lose it, just come undone, with no idea what that would lead to. Living in the temporary home added to the sense of instability. It was wonderful to have a private place. We knew we could have easily ended up in a shelter somewhere, but here we were in a brand-new home. Pretty soon, the twins started trying to tear it down with their kicking. We warned the builder what might happen to the model home, telling him ahead of time that there could be damage. The insurance company was alerted to the potential problems. And, sure enough, the walls had to be rebuilt after we'd been there only nine months.

The sad fact was, the fire caused the twins to be more volatile than ever. Every time I drove the family to the house as it was being rebuilt, Austin began punching himself. He would do it so violently I'd have to pull the car over to try to stop him. I had to move him to the front seat so I could hold and restrain his hands. Even then he'd wrestle against me as I tried to drive.

These weren't little slaps to the cheek. He punched himself as hard as he could, right in the face, hitting his nose and eyes, while shouting, "Mama almost died, Mama almost died." Maybe he was trying to punish himself, or maybe hurting himself was his way of communicating all the frustration he had built up inside. It was a savage attack on himself, and his face became bruised and swollen, like he'd been in a prizefight.

I kept telling him that I was all right, nobody got hurt, and nobody blamed him. But every time he saw the house, he felt guilty. Dr. Reid said that she could see the anguish that Austin built up inside, and it deeply affected his behavior for quite a while. It caused a serious regression in just about every aspect of his development.

Christian's trauma was more internal. He withdrew even further and continued to lose weight, at one point weighing one hundred pounds less than Austin. Christian had always been best when operating on a strictly regulated schedule and routine. Being uprooted and placed in a different house disrupted everything he knew. During that time, so many of his obsessive-compulsive behaviors worsened. He would sometimes freeze in place or be unable to get himself out of a room—taking a step forward and a step back—and then be overcome by the anxiety of it. His mood darkened, too. For a while, he repeatedly asked Austin to poke him in the back with a pencil. Thankfully, Austin didn't do it. They were both frustrated and angry, and they took out their feelings on the house and on themselves, particularly by biting their arms. We had to wrap their arms with bandages because they were biting themselves so much that they wouldn't heal.

Jonathan also fought inner conflicts during this time. He'd been so heroic during the fire; his fast actions had been vital in saving the other kids' lives—mine, too, for that matter. But he also had lived through a potentially lethal experience and had been uprooted from everything he knew. He was still a midteen, and the fire, relocation, and uncertainty of everything added to all the other social challenges a typical teen faces. At times Jonathan was angry that his brothers made his life so different from those of his friends, and then he felt awful for being so angry at brothers who he knew were needy and couldn't help themselves. He started closing himself off, just finding ways to not have to deal with the mayhem—spending more time at his friends' houses and retreating to his room for privacy.

Little Isabella never wanted to be out of arm's reach from me. It was traumatic for a two-year-old who had only been with our family for a few months. We think about the fire every year around her birthday.

When your life and the lives of your children are endangered, it is the definition of an existential moment. We went from trying to make things better and finding solutions to just trying to hold ourselves together. The therapies and programs that had helped the twins gain ground had to be put on hold. I couldn't get my brain back into homeschooling again. All the energy we had spent on researching and trying new therapies had to be funneled in a different direction. Life in temporary housing, rebuilding the home, healing emotionally—we were all worn down by everything that had happened. We faced our typical chaos every day in the home, but beyond that, we all seemed to feel a deep hurt. Everyone was so upset by the fire. Everyone's patience was short. We were all emotionally bruised and tender.

We decided to put the boys back in school rather than homeschooling, and they entered middle school special education classes. I just wasn't up to teaching again.

As we began to see our home come back together, our family seemed to be falling apart. I once got a call from the school because Christian was stuck in one position for so long he couldn't move. Another time I was called to school to get Austin because he wasn't feeling well. He ended up having a seizure so bad that he froze up, and I had to call 911.

Through all of this, we tried to remember to be thankful. People we didn't even know had jumped in to help us. That outpouring of generosity was so gratifying and uplifting that it brought me to tears. Still, I think we all were a lot more skeptical about how we looked at our future.

Austin, Christian, Isabella, and Jonathan.

CHAPTER 14

BIG BROTHER

ANA

Having talked to so many other families living with autism, I found it a fairly common perception that the "neurotypical" siblings get less attention. Because parents can become so focused on the child or children with greater needs, they have trouble finding the energy to spend enough time with the other siblings. And even when they can parcel out the time, how much do they have to give?

When he got into his teens, Jonathan started to decline offers whenever we suggested he bring friends to the house. The place was a disaster, with the holes in the walls and all the commotion. Nobody knew when one of the twins might have a dramatic meltdown. Especially when he was young, Jonathan didn't know how to explain the twins' behavior to his friends. It was easier for him to just go to their houses.

Jonathan has always known he shouldn't use the boys' autism as an excuse or a crutch, or a diversion from living up to his own potential. In fact, I remember only one time when Jonathan expected somebody to feel sorry for him.

He was probably thirteen or so, a stage when I suspect many teenagers complain about how difficult their lives are. He began complaining about how unfair everything was. I had zero patience for that kind of talk. I backed him against the wall and told him, "Don't come at me with that, God chose us to be a family, we've got to stick together and get through this as a family. That's what families do!" I'm sure I stunned him with such an emphatic response. Maybe it was too much, maybe I wasn't as understanding as I should have been. He was only a young boy. But none of our lives were going to get easier by complaining. That was the last time he had a little pity party for himself.

I remember one day when the twins were little and I was exhausted and drained and an emotional wreck. I sat on the stairs near the kitchen, put my head in my hands, and cried my eyes out. Jonathan came up and hugged me and said, "It's going to be okay, Mom, we're going to be okay. Everything will work out." It was such a role reversal, the young kid comforting the sobbing mother when I was having a little pity party for myself! I felt like everything seemed to be falling apart, but Jonathan was assuring me we'd be okay. In that moment, I knew what a good man he would turn out to be and how amazingly mature he had already become.

Because I was home watching the twins most of the time, I didn't get to see many of Jonathan's sports events. Curt would always give me reports on how he was doing and what happened during his games, but I wished I could have been there. Jonathan and I discovered other ways to spend time together and connect, though. Whenever *The Cosby Show* was on, we'd lie down on the bed and watch it, just the two of us. That was our special thirty minutes together. We laughed the whole time.

I think we both tried to live vicariously through the Cosby family—if only for half an hour at a time.

The twins have always looked up to Jonathan and wanted to be like their big brother. When Jonathan was at Penn State, Austin would say of him, "He's a grown-up . . . he goes to college." The twins saw Jonathan progress from high school and then go to college. Austin told me that once they graduated from high school, he would go to Penn State just like Jonathan. It was a hard realization that it was something the twins would not be able to do.

Jonathan graduated from Penn State in 2016 and works at a Portland radio station, so he's around home enough now to spend time with the twins and Isabella. He'll say, "If you need to go do something, go ahead, I can take care of them." He's still a big help with the boys.

CURT

There probably should be more studies made of the trials of "autism's siblings," or there should be some support group established for them. In a lot of cases, they have to mature faster and become more responsible and independent. The teenage years, especially, have to be a tough time for many of them. Kids can be very blunt and somewhat mean-spirited. I think Jonathan's not wanting other kids to come over to the house was a way of protecting his brothers. It also saved him from having to explain everything.

Where Jonathan missed out the most, I think, is in not having the chance at a more typical brother-type relationship with Austin and Christian. That camaraderie was missing, and I'm sorry he couldn't have it. My brother Robert and I competed in sports beside each other growing up. That time together was extremely important to shaping who I am today. As my father had done for me when I was young, I connected with Jonathan through sports and volunteered to coach some of his teams. I jumped in when he was at Camas High. I didn't directly coach him; I coached the running backs, and he was a receiver, which was probably a good thing since I would never want to play favorites and it might have put us in uncomfortable positions. I still knew a little about catching the ball, so I'd tell him a few things now and then—some of them he listened to and other times he'd give me a look like I didn't have a clue what I was talking about. That didn't matter. We were able to spend that time together, the two of us, and I really enjoyed it.

I was so impressed by him and the way he matured. It was really something to see how he grew during that time. Life in our house wasn't easy for him, but he became an all-area wide receiver and earned a scholarship to Penn State. I was particularly proud that he graduated from Penn State with a degree in broadcast journalism.

CHAPTER 15

A LIGHT IN THE DARK

JONATHAN

I had nightmares of that day for a long time.

I almost never missed school, but bronchitis laid me up, so I was allowed to stay home that day. I was resting and watching television from the bed in my parents' room when I heard Austin scream. "Help! Fire!"

Of course, I thought it was a joke, but when I got up to check, it was no joke; a fire was already engulfing the twins' room, so there was no way of saving the house. I quickly grabbed my little sister, Isabella, and tried to get everybody in the car to get away from the fire.

When I finally found him, Austin tried to tell me he was sorry. In my anger, I told him it was his fault, and I punched him in the stomach as hard as I could. I felt like a monster. I looked into his eyes and could tell he knew it wasn't one of our "play fights." Eventually, we hopped in my mom's car and backed out of the garage. My mother was in tears as we all watched our house go up in flames.

But I had no tears—just pure rage, frustration, and hatred for my brother. My brothers often made me angry, but this was different. This was an anger where I did not want to associate myself with them as brothers any longer. My rage in that moment had been building, of course. I always felt alone in one way or another because of their autism and the fact that my brothers weren't like "normal" brothers. As I watched the fire destroy my house, I blamed all of it on my autistic brother who was trying to reenact a Disney movie.

The earliest I remember knowing that my brothers were a little bit different was when I went to visit one of my friends and I saw him playing with his brother. It gave me this empty feeling. Why can't I communicate with Austin and Christian like that? Why does this have to happen to me? Even when I was very young, these questions were running through my mind.

I remember asking my mother what was wrong with them. She said that they had a mental disorder. A mental disorder? Like something is wrong with their brains? She tried to explain autism to me; they both had it, and no, it wasn't a bad thing, but they weren't like me. I was crushed. I didn't really understand at the time, but it made me feel as if I had to grow up faster.

When I got older, I hated for friends to come over to my house. I wouldn't allow it. I was ashamed of my brothers, and I didn't want other kids to see what went on in our house every day. I don't think my mom really noticed this. She asked a couple of times why I never had anybody over, but I didn't want to tell her that I couldn't stand to be at home. I coped with the whole family situation by getting away from it, hanging out with friends. After our house was renovated, they gave me the third floor to myself; I really needed that to have my own space, and I could lock the door and get away from everything.

There were times when I thought, *I don't want to be in this family anymore.* As a teenager, I was pretty tight with rage. The twins were going through puberty and acting up. One minute they'd be all right, and the next minute they'd be doing things you couldn't believe. Austin would bite Christian and Christian would bite himself, and then Austin would bite me. It was brutal. I don't know how to describe it. It was like watching a horror movie.

To this day I have bad memories, and I get anxiety and I kind of freak out a little bit. I'd see a fire on TV or hear about a fire, and I'd cringe a little bit. It's a deadly element.

For me, autism was like this giant monkey on my back that wouldn't let go, and I mean really, it wouldn't let go. I could feel the judgment people had toward me and my family. Maybe it was some kind of paranoia on my part, I'm not sure, but I always felt that people judged me by my brothers' condition, and I hated it. I had a few friends who understood my family situation. If you were my friend, I considered you my brother. My friends became my family, and my family became this weird thing that I did not want to be a part of. It was how I coped.

It took me time to mature out of that negative point of view. I wasn't the greatest son or brother in the world, I'll admit that, but I grew out of it. There was so much going on and so much stress. Now when I see the twins, we're good. They are my brothers. Understanding what the twins were going through took time; it came with age and maturity.

I tell others who have brothers or sisters with autism that you have to stick through it, and it's tough. God puts you on this earth for a purpose, and that may be for you to be a good brother to somebody with autism.

You never know what's happening in everybody's lives behind their closed doors. You have to keep that in mind; you have to give people the respect they deserve. I would say the experience of having brothers with autism made me more patient. I'm very patient with people now—reserved and patient.

It took me a while to learn this. It wasn't easy. But I don't have the nightmares anymore.

CHAPTER 16

FINDING OUR WAY

ANA

It seemed like we were always in one of those dreams where you're trying to find your way out of a maze, or there's one important thing you're looking for that is always just out of reach.

Autism is a neurological disorder, but I agree with those doctors who believe a key to treating it is taking care of the gut. Like many kids with autism, our twins deal with candida, a condition that can affect digestive health and nutrient absorption. It has to do with body chemistry and the ability to flush toxins from their systems. Christian and Austin seem to be more susceptible to the effects of toxins. The best way to control toxins is by improving the quality of the food they eat.

I got very serious about this approach. We feed them balanced meals of healthy food to try to limit their intake of toxins. I shop at several stores three times a week for organic fruits and vegetables and grass-fed organic meats. Over time, the whole family went to a diet that is mostly gluten-free, casein-free, dairy-free, and grain-free. Curt used to always add "flavor-free" to that list, but he finally got on board with our eating healthy.

I prepare all their meals myself, every day, sometimes spending five hours a day in preparation. Yes, it's a lot of work, but I enjoy it. It's something I can do that seems to have a positive effect. I feel very blessed that I can stay home and cook for my family. I know so many parents with special needs children don't have that option.

Curt jokes with me that I would like to get a cow so I could have total control over the food that comes into this house. Yes, I'd love that. And chickens, too, and vegetables we could grow organically ourselves. I believe so strongly in the value of a healthy diet because when we chart their food intake, healthier food correlates to improved behavior. Some of our modified-diet approach was under doctors' recommendations, and some was a result of our own trial and error, or suggestions from others who had kids on the spectrum with digestive problems. The strict dietary regimen is not a cure, but we've committed to trying to minimize some of the worst behavior. If healthy food is a way to improve the twins' lives without pills or drugs, then it's worth it, even if it's just by a few percent.

When the twins were really young, we didn't know any of this, so they ate the typical diet of American kids—including potato chips and foods with red dye No. 40. That dye is not allowed in some countries in Europe because of the effects it can have on people with certain sensitivities. When we got them off the red dye, both Austin and Christian became less hyper.

We spent years going through what doctors call "elimination" diets: eliminating certain foods or ingredients from the twins' diet for a period of time and trying to track changes in their behavior at the time of each exclusion. We kept food journals and charted everything they ate. We monitored practically every bite, and with the help of the therapists, we concluded that Red No. 40 was one of the things that made them particularly hyperactive.

It became obvious that finding the best diets for the individual boys made a difference for them. By preparing every meal from scratch, and being with the boys all day every day, I developed a good feeling for their reactions to different foods and ingredients, but it's hardly an exact science.

Christian's health declined when he hit his teens. He was getting thinner, scary thin, with dark circles around his eyes. Tests revealed he was malnourished even though he was getting plenty of healthy food. Dr. John Green III suggested we try dietary changes, specifically going without gluten and casein proteins. We had tried that earlier, shortly after the boys were diagnosed, but it frustrated the whole family because there were so few options at the time, and they tended to be flavorless. The changes were met with resistance. First, it was a battle with the twins because kids with autism can get stuck in the habit of eating certain favorite foods, and deviating from them could mean dealing with meltdowns for days. Our boys usually wanted no changes from a routine of chicken nuggets, French fries, and macaroni and cheese. Many parents just can't keep up with the challenges of finding healthy things that kids will eat.

Christian was so sickly, though, it seemed worth another try. We found new cookbooks and a wider variety of healthy recipes—and the whole family bought in, including a reluctant Curt. And Christian rallied again.

Now, we've given up grains, going almost completely "caveman." The boys like certain foods that are good for them: rice and beans and chicken . . . gluten-free spaghetti, meat loaf, hamburgers, and a lot of vegetables. Sometimes I try to sneak vegetables into the spaghetti sauce and meat loaf for those extra servings. Breakfast might be sausage and fruit, lunch will be rice and beans and chicken, and dinner a different meat. Snacks are fruits and nuts.

Once we were fully committed, accepting the change was easier than I thought. All of us benefited from a healthier diet. Funny that it was Curt, not the twins, who needed the most convincing to make the switch.

CURT

I was not excited about the changes to our diet. Why did I need to be part of the boys' therapy? At the time that we decided to make the change, organic and healthy food really was not very tasty. Secondly, I didn't want to give up sweets . . . or fried chicken or pizza. I mean, food was something that felt like a pleasant reward at a time when other parts of our lives were far less rewarding.

But I had to be willing to adapt, right? I needed to be part of the team and be on board with the program. I liked to gripe about it for show for a while, but I do feel healthier because of it.

Obviously, it made life a lot more difficult for Ana, having to cook every meal every single day—never being able to pop in to a fast-food place for meals. But it was a decision she made for the good of the boys. She would cook twenty-four hours a day if she thought it would help them a little bit.

I get a few cheats every now and then, but I mostly stick to the program. I drew the line at getting our own cow and chickens, though.

ANA

Austin's anxiety after the fire demonstrated his ability to internalize guilt. This means there are times when he understands consequences. This wasn't always the case. Initially, when the fire started, he certainly had to be scared, right? So we presumed that laughing about the fire was the way he released emotions in the moment. When he had time to absorb what had happened, and connect the action of lighting the fire to the result of the house burning, he began to understand the real danger of what he'd done. And he was remorseful. Too remorseful for his own good, in fact, as he started harming himself when reminded of the damage.

As they've grown into young men, we have found ways to reinforce good behavior and make the twins recognize the cost of bad behavior. It's an important tool we didn't always have. For example, like so many young adults, they love their iPads for watching videos, and having those devices gives us leverage for teaching purposes. Whenever Austin breaks a rule, Curt likes to tell him, "That will cost you, my friend," and he takes away his tablet for a while. When that happens a time or two, Austin makes the connection and whatever rule he might want to break again isn't worth the loss of his device.

We know the twins don't fully grasp some deep emotional concepts, like death or grief. At least they don't show it at times when you think they might. Austin will sometimes tell us the year that Walt Disney died, and add, "He's not getting up." I've started to think the twins' idea of death is like in the movies. In the movies, the character dies and you can rewind it and watch it again. Magically, he or she comes back to life.

We really sensed the disconnect when Lucky, our Labrador retriever, died. We told the twins that Lucky was going to heaven and they should say goodbye to him. They said a quick "goodbye" and walked away. The rest of us were bawling, but they were very unemotional about it.

In 2004, a close family friend, Jerry Rivera, passed away. The boys called him "Uncle Jerry." The twins saw him when he was sick and prayed for him with us. They knew he was important to our family. After Jerry died, we visited his widow, Donna. It was a delicate time, of course, but Austin said to her, "No more Uncle Jerry. He's dead!" It probably would have sounded insensitive from other kids his age and not in keeping with the seriousness of the moment. I was afraid Donna would start crying, but instead she just responded with, "Yes, Austin, Uncle Jerry is in heaven." She understood that Austin perceives some serious things in matter-of-fact terms. The boys loved him and always were happy to see him, but they showed no emotion about his death.

Through the years, they've seen me crying many times. While Jonathan often would comfort me, the twins might simply say something like "Mommy's sad" and go about their business with little or no emotional connection being made. Dr. Green told us that he believes the twins may have deeper emotions that simply don't get expressed. Maybe they just don't know how. Even the nonverbal kids on the spectrum, he said, will suddenly do something that shows they know what you're saying, and they have an opinion on it. Our boys sometimes communicate better than we thought they could. But we mostly just have to be attuned to what their actions are telling us. Austin and Christian do not usually have objections to being touched or hugged. It's one of the stereotypes of ASD they don't follow. We kiss and hug and tell each of them we love them all the time, and they tend to return our affection. So, we feel sure the twins understand the concept of family and togetherness. In fact, I suspect we got more displays of love from them than we would from a neurotypical child their age—especially as they got into their late teens.

Austin had an interesting response once when I wasn't feeling well and probably got a little overexerted. I passed out, and Austin found me on the floor. It was pretty clear that he must have thought I was dead because when I came to, Austin started yelling, "She's alive, she's alive!"

"Yes, honey," I told him, "I just passed out."

He got confused and asked, "Mom, you just passed gas?"

I had to laugh. "No, Austin, I passed out, I didn't pass gas."

"Whew," he said, very relieved.

There's a saying in the autism community: *Normal* is a setting on your washer—that's the only *normal* you're going to get.

But there are a number of common behaviors we've heard about from other families affected by autism. Many other kids on the spectrum also have a curious obsession with all things Disney. On the twins' first visit to a speech pathologist, they had virtually no functional vocabulary, but they could clearly pronounce some multisyllabic names of Disney characters. We had assumed it was an affinity specific to our twins, but discovered it's not just a Warner trait.

Why the passion for Disney? Curt thinks the kids like the colorful animation and the pleasant musical soundtracks. We've asked doctors and other parents of children on the spectrum, and no one seems to have a solid theory. Apparently, it's not only common, but has been unwavering over the years. Even into their twenties, our twins continue their fascination with animated programming—especially Disney.

I hear them throughout the house during the day, repeating the movie dialogues. They seem to take some comfort in knowing what's coming next; the action and the dialogue never change. Plus, most of the movies have fairly predictable plots with recognizable characters. Our kids don't like surprises, so perhaps the Disney movies are perfect in that way.

One afternoon, when Isabella was crying in the kitchen, I was stunned when Austin came in and asked, *"Qu'est-ce qui se passe?"* He had been on his iPad watching a Disney movie in French on YouTube. His pronunciation and usage were perfect.

Austin can provide any detail of every Disney movie from the last decade or more. Producer, director, voice actors, anything. His recall of this information is instant and thorough. But he can't tell you how many quarters make a dollar.

I've read that some parents have been able to improve their connection with their children by imitating Disney characters, but Austin will shut you down in a hurry and tell you to go away if you try to act like a Disney character.

I knew Austin was in a phase where we had to keep a close eye on him when he started listing every instance in the movies when the Little Mermaid and Pinocchio disobeyed their fathers. He noticed that the characters had fun being a little rebellious. We had to teach him that things worked differently for real little boys than for children in the animated movies. That was an example of our learning to spot potential dangers and proactively derail them.

The only time the boys apply Disney references to us is when they're angry. They will sometimes call us the names of Disney villains; they've called Curt "Scar" a few times—the antagonist from *The Lion King*. And I've been called Cruella De Vil, Evil Queen, and Maleficent.

I was certainly the Evil Queen to Austin when I decided I'd had enough of their focus on Disney movies and demanded they find other means of entertainment. Why? First, I got the idea they'd be better off if we diverted them onto some other visual stimuli that might broaden their learning experiences. Second, I was really, really tired of hearing Disney quotes all day and all night, every day of my life. But as much as I tried to interest them in other things, they kept pressing me for Disney. So, I decided to fill a couple of big bags with all the Disney VHS tapes and take them along with the VHS player to donate to Goodwill. They watched me as I packed everything up. There were years' worth of movies. I reminded them I had given them the chance to watch other things. I brought Austin and Christian with me when I delivered it all to Goodwill. I was sure it was the only way to minimize their obsession. If they didn't like it, they'd learn to get over it in time.

When I told Curt what we had done that day, he shook his head and said, "Bad idea, very, very bad idea."

No kidding. Within about two days, I was back at Goodwill trying to buy everything back. The boys reacted with far more hostility than I had expected. They made our lives pretty miserable. Every day, fairly constantly since 2009, Christian gives me a dirty look and starts chanting "VHS, VHS, VHS." He'll never let the Evil Queen forget. We're still piecing the collection back together.

CURT

The folks at Disney are aware of their appeal to ASD kids, and they've tried to work out ways to accommodate their needs at theme parks. But the crowds and bustle make it a challenge, and the constant sensory stimulation can be tough on kids with ASD. On our trip to Disneyland, Austin begged to go on Space Mountain. We gave it a try. I wish we had a picture of them coming down the chute. Christian had the biggest smile on his face, and Austin was in high terror, hiding his face with his hands. One in sheer joy, the other in terror.

CHAPTER 17

TRIALS AND ERRORS

ANA

I tend to operate mostly on the instincts I've developed with the boys over the years. Curt, on the other hand, is very analytical. He likes to consider the goal and then plot ways to minimize drama and maximize results. He wants to have a game plan. It's probably his sports background, or maybe his experience running a business. Having this approach makes great sense when you know all the variables. But there were no playbooks for the life we led. We ended up going by trial and error most of the time and had to come up with our own set of operating procedures as we went.

When the kids were younger, they demanded to see the new Disney movie the second it was released. But that's when every other little kid wants to see those movies, too, and a crowded theater can be a tough

environment for our boys. Crowds mean noise and stress and sometimes the uncomfortable closeness of strangers. Our adaptation? We'd
get tickets to the earliest showings and arrive at the theater early enough
that we could get seats where other people don't normally like to sit.
We followed the same approach when checking into a hotel. If they
could give us a room at the far end of the emptiest floor, everybody's
stay would be quieter.

We also used this tactic at restaurants. Mostly, I cooked everything
at home, but when we went out for a meal, it was at off-peak times,
and we talked to the host as soon as we got there. We explained our
situation and asked for a corner booth or a quiet section. We added
details, too. I'd tell them, You might see a man leading two full-grown
boys to the bathroom by their hands. This is their father, and he's just
watching out for them.

I would have loved to have been able to take the twins to Brazil to
spend time with my father before he passed. But imagine a twenty-four-
hour trip, in the tight confines of a plane, with me not being able to go
to the bathroom. I couldn't take both of them with me to the lavatory,
or leave them both sitting there by themselves when I went. For Curt
to come along and help with the twins, he'd have had to take the time
off work, and the entire family would have had to fly, adding to the
expense and stress.

We've managed some shorter flights, though, and found that the
best way to start off a trip is with a great deal of preparation and communication. Curt is brilliant at this. Curt goes to the airport several days
before the flight and explains the boys' situation, exploring ways they
might get through security a little faster or board the plane when there
is less of a rush. If we have to get to the airport much earlier than most
other families would, well, that's fine; anything that will reduce the
stress is worth it. Informed in advance, the airlines and security people
are usually accommodating. Clearly, with the rate of autism on the rise,
our situation is becoming more and more common.

When we have to fly, I make a habit of telling everybody in the rows nearby, "I have two kids with autism. I promise we're going to do the very best we can, but you might hear some noise." I'm usually dreading the flight, but I always put a big smile on my face and am as pleasant as I can be. People tend to be more understanding of chaos when you explain it in advance and they know you're going to do your best.

Understanding, however, is not universal. We know that's just how it is. Again, awareness is growing, and that has to help in the future.

For the *Disney on Ice* visit at the Rose Garden Arena in Portland, I parked in the adjoining concrete garage—a cavernous place with an echo. Austin was particularly excited about the show. And when he discovered the echo in the garage, he started yelling, "Hello . . . hello" to listen to it repeat from a distance. I thought, *Oh, well, we are in the garage*, and it was nearly empty because we were so early, so no harm. I had learned by then that I couldn't just say no to everything they do, plus, this was probably the first time he'd heard an echo.

It turned out that we were not quite alone in the garage. A lady came up to me and said, "You should tell your kids not to be yelling so much, it bothers people." I tried to explain, nicely: It was my fault that I didn't try to stop him because I didn't think it would bother anybody. He has autism and . . . She interrupted and yelled at me, "I don't care what their problems are, you need to do better as a parent!"

I stood there and bit my tongue as she walked away. It was evident that she didn't understand anything about autism, and she surely wasn't interested in listening to my explanations. Yes, it was hurtful. Sometimes, inside, I feel like telling people off. But I don't.

Sporting events are usually out of the question as crowds can put a lot of pressure on the boys and make them uncomfortable. Although Curt loved his time with the Seahawks and still follows the team closely, he hasn't been able to nurture that connection with the franchise because of the demands at home and challenges of bringing the twins to games. Seahawks general manager John Schneider and his wife, Traci, are very familiar with autism. They've established Ben's Fund, an autism fund-raiser named after their son, who is on the spectrum. Seahawks fans can be proud to cheer for a franchise run by people who are so aware and charitable.

John and Traci once invited our whole family to watch a game at CenturyLink Field. The Seahawks were amazing to us, very welcoming and gracious. They had invited us up a number of times, but we could so rarely go. It's not that we're trying to hide our boys. We love our boys. We're proud of them. We just always feared that all the people and the noise could trigger behavior that was unpredictable or dangerous. But when the Schneiders arranged seats for us in one of the Seahawks' boxes, we decided to give it a try.

The experience was too much for Christian. He had his hands over his ears the whole time, and I held him pretty much constantly to give him a sense of comfort. As it is so often with these two, the other brother had the opposite response. Austin did perfectly fine. He had a terrific time.

CURT

We tend to have our own strengths with the kids. Ana is the one who's the best at diagnosing behaviors and figuring out what they mean and how we might adjust our approach to deal with their changing conditions. She's really adept at finding out what's bothering the boys. She's the master chef, too, tinkering with their food to find the right ingredients.

I'm often the one trying to decide how we deal with some of the larger logistics, looking ahead, planning, finding ways to avoid potential threats or complications. The twins' behavior is more predictable now that they're older, so my role has gotten easier, but the possibility of either of them wandering off carries different risks now that the boys are more mobile. They are full-grown adults, but unable to explain to anyone who they are, where they live, or that they suffer from a disorder.

Austin, given his outgoing nature, could be seen as a threat to somebody. I imagine him rushing up to a policeman and getting in his face, as he does, and shouting at him—which is Austin's normal tone of voice. He might only be trying to be friendly and introduce himself, but just about anybody could see that as aggressive behavior. What would happen if Austin failed to answer the officer's questions or follow his instructions? We fear that a situation like that could go very badly.

When the boys were younger, we were asked to leave when we tried to eat at a sports club. Austin screamed a couple times; we tried to get him toned down, of course, but they kicked us out. It made me angry, sure. It felt like they were saying, *You guys are bad parents, you need to make them behave.* At the time, we were still figuring out ways to cope with such situations. Now, when we're out, we'll see people look at us and nod, as if to acknowledge, *Oh, right, spectrum.* We don't consider that insensitive. It's far preferable to the responses we had in the past. It likely means that people know somebody with autism and will be more understanding if one of the twins starts displaying some disruptive behaviors. We're encouraged by the growth in this kind of understanding and tolerance. It makes it easier for families with children on the spectrum to get out and be more social these days.

Ana and I always try to be considerate of others in public. Everyone else in the theater paid for the movie just like we did, or they're out to dinner at a restaurant to have a good time just like we are. We want the twins to have as many positive experiences as possible, but we don't want to invade others' space and affect their experience, either. So often, we just don't know what will present a problem for the boys. Behaviors can change with their moods or the kind of day they've had. We recently were going for a little celebration at Red Robin, a place the twins are usually really happy and excited to go to. The servers there always have a good attitude when interacting with our family. But on this day we'd been busy running around, and the twins were dragging a bit. We could tell they weren't feeling their best. Before we even went inside, we decided to ask them if they wanted to just leave and come back some other day. They said yes. We ate at home, and the evening was calm. We've learned to watch for their signals and stay out of situations that might be better avoided.

CHAPTER 18

THE COSTS

ANA

Any number of doctors have told me I needed to take better care of myself. That's certainly the advice I pass along to other parents of children with autism. But most mothers I talk to just don't think that way. They don't focus on their own needs, certainly not above those of their children. It's like when you hear those announcements on the airplane: "If the oxygen masks come down, put yours on first before you help your children." You know what? No mother will do that. They think of their children first; they'll put the child's mask on first every time. Every time.

So when my children couldn't sleep, I thought that I shouldn't sleep, either. If they were having troubles, I needed to be there to take care of them. I know that Curt and I both put our own health lower on the priorities list. That, along with the long-term stress, contributed to some chronic health problems for me.

A few years ago I started having a low-grade fever and a sore throat, and feeling extremely fatigued. I would wake up in the morning and drag myself out of bed, already feeling tired. I would make breakfast for everybody and get them out to school, and then I would lie down on the couch until it was time to pick up Isabella from preschool. I would feed her lunch, turn the TV on for her, and go back to the couch. At two thirty, the boys would come home, and the dinner routine would start. After dinner, I was ready for bed again.

If I tried to walk even a mile for exercise, I would need to spend the next three days on the couch. This feeling lasted for months, and I felt worthless. All of a sudden, I had no choice but to pay attention to my health. My doctor diagnosed chronic fatigue syndrome and put me on a regimen of supplements. Combined with going on the strict diet with the boys, that helped me rebuild my energy.

The symptoms would return sporadically, though, and when I started feeling numbness in my face and hands, a doctor checked for multiple sclerosis. A CT scan returned normal results, so the neurologist cited the continued stress as the probable cause for the symptoms. I was sent to a therapist for help in coping. The psychologist was great because she had a son with autism and could relate to the pressures. She told me that I had chronic stress, anxiety, and depression, and needed to find a way to relax.

I knew the doctor was being serious about prescribing rest, but I got a pretty good laugh out of that. Relax? I fear I've forgotten how. Even if we could get away, I'd never stop worrying and thinking about the kids. It was asking me to set aside two decades' worth of conditioning. That's a hard pattern to break.

I've always worried so much about Curt's health, starting with the carnage he suffered in the NFL. Of course we're paying attention to the studies of CTE—the degenerative brain disorder that so many former

NFL players have developed. There's far more concern about concussions now than when he played, which is a much-needed development. They've instituted some rules to protect players, and the game has changed, which Curt believes will benefit players. They deserve better protection. When he was playing, doctors didn't consider the long-term effects of concussions. He recalled times when a doctor would ask him how many fingers he was holding up, and if he got the right number, he was deemed ready for action. They might give him a sniff of an ammonia capsule and send him back in the game.

In 2010, Curt was diagnosed with Graves' disease, which affects thyroid function. After a couple months of naturopathic treatment, though, the symptoms subsided. We've both had to take more time to listen to our bodies and pay attention to what they are telling us as we age.

CURT

As far as the literal dollar costs of autism are concerned, the Centers for Disease Control and Prevention reported in 2017 that the additional cost of raising a child on the lower end of the ASD spectrum was more than $21,000 a year. That's for therapies and treatments and services. And for one child, of course, not twins. We've never let cost be a prime factor when we were making decisions concerning the twins' care. There was nothing spared to try to get them healthy.

In the early days, it felt like everything we did to try to help them was an uphill battle. Education, medications, social issues—there were no services or systems set up to help those with ASD. After the boys' diagnosis, the behavioral therapy was totally out of pocket. And with two boys, that meant eighty hours a week of intensive therapy. Now many insurance companies are starting to pay for some autism treatments, but the coverage varies by state.

Still, much of the twins' treatment was naturopathic, and that always has been out of pocket. The special diets and supplements add to that, and that's not taking into account the costs of home repairs we've faced for years.

So, yes, we've spent a lot of our personal resources trying to do the best we could for our kids. We've got great sympathy for those families with limited resources. Autism doesn't care if you have money or not. It's painful to think of the people who can't do all the things we were able to do in terms of treatments and therapies. Ana and I talk about it all the time.

It's another reason why we'll never stop trying to find answers and a cure for this disorder. If effective treatments could be pinpointed, the costs would likely come down for everybody. And there certainly would be less money spent on things that didn't work.

The costs of this disorder aren't just to the families, either. School programs are more comprehensive now, but when the twins were younger, schools weren't prepared for the demands. I'm still not really sure how school districts stand in regard to handling the growing number of students on the spectrum. I don't know if there are enough special education teachers and therapists out there to handle the demand. The cold fact, which we all know, is that it's going to cost a lot of money to get anything done. I felt at times over the years that school administrators were trying to learn as they went, which, in a lot of ways, was exactly what we were trying to do, too.

As the twins age out of the social systems geared to aid those with disabilities, we have to start thinking about long-term adult autism care. I tried to be smart with my football money, and I went right to work after retirement, feeling that I always needed to be bringing in a paycheck. I'm glad. We're certainly reaching a stage where we have a lot of planning to do for the twins, and money very definitely has become a concern. In the spring of 2015, we sold our family home—the one that had been rebuilt after the fire—to downsize in an effort to fund living arrangements for Austin's and Christian's adult lives.

After we got to know Helyn Rosemurgy, the autism counselor who first got us started with the ABA therapy, she told Ana that when she starts talking to families of the newly diagnosed, she tries to delicately get a sense of how well-off they are financially. It's not being overly personal, it's a very practical matter. Treatments are expensive, and a lot of people are forced into making very difficult decisions. We were extremely blessed that we could afford for Ana to stay home to take care of the boys' treatments, as well as cook and clean and care for them. I don't know how people without help can do it. This is very challenging in so many ways, but then it can become so expensive in addition to everything else. It's painful to think how hard it can get for so many families.

Ana and I have talked to many parents who struggle, and we hear the stories all too frequently. Many families end up charging therapies on credit cards, others get second mortgages or cash in their retirement accounts. Having to deal with those stresses on top of everything is almost unimaginable. Even with the financial advantages we had early in our marriage, life with autism brings a change in perspective. I've seen it with Ana. When she looks at a pair of jeans in a store, she'll check the price tag and compare the cost to how many months of vitamins for the twins it would buy. She ends up putting a lot of things back on the rack.

CHAPTER 19

ACCENTUATING THE POSITIVES

CURT

Many of the really dramatic things we've been through in our lives sound so negative. They're the parts of our story that people will remember, but I think they paint an incomplete picture.

Sometimes the best parts of being parents are the quiet and close and warm times—just being together. We didn't get many of those in the early days. And the memories of those moments as a family tend to get overshadowed by the trips to the emergency room, the stitches, the 911 calls, and the sleepless nights.

When you are dealing with a flooded bathroom because a toy has been flushed down the toilet, or you've spent all night patching holes in the wall only to see more the next day, it's hard to remember to go around counting your blessings. I confess: I got overwhelmed by the negative at times. But focusing solely on those things isn't fair to the boys.

I love that they try so hard, especially since life is often tough and frustrating for them. Imagine having health troubles and pain and not being able to tell anybody about them.

Austin and Christian are growing and changing in a lot of ways that are positive. They're not hurting themselves as often, and they're not nearly as destructive.

There's no way to quantify this, but it just seems that Austin and Christian are smiling more. They're happier. There's less pain. That's what I want for them. I love seeing them interacting with each other and being able to get out of the house and experience life a little more. We no longer have to be watching them every second. These are the things we envisioned for them.

There came a point where we realized that the absence of negatives is a very positive thing. That perspective helped us find joy more easily.

Austin is the perfect example. He's such a character with so much humor and often makes us curious about his unique behavior. For instance, he'll walk into the kitchen, get ice cubes from the freezer, put them in his pants pocket, and then walk off. Why? Because he's Austin, and Austin's world is a very interesting place. We can appreciate that better now.

He has so much personality, and he so desperately wants to communicate with people. But it's not easy for him. If you've ever watched *Seinfeld*, you'll know what I mean when I say that Austin is a "close talker." He'll get right up in your space and start talking really loudly and won't back off. Whenever we're at a store checking out, Austin always wants to introduce himself to the clerks. "Hey, mister, what's your name? Mister, what's your name? I'm Austin." It's always with good intentions, and he's always got a big smile on his face. You can tell in that situation that he's just trying to get to know somebody. But some folks aren't quite sure about it when he gets up so close and starts yelling at them. He can go all day asking questions. It can be distracting if you're trying to get something done, but it's also evidence that he's trying so hard to learn things.

Ana told me once about Austin trying to communicate with a bagger at one of the local grocery stores who is hearing impaired. She tried to explain to Austin that the boy couldn't hear him, so Austin got up really close and yelled at him. The bagger understood that Austin has autism and tried to sign a bit to him. Austin thought he was "stimming."

Austin loves Jonathan and wants to be just like him, so he trains really hard in the gym. Jonathan was always very fit due to playing football and other sports, so Austin does quite a bit of CrossFit and gets a good workout. His trainer says that Austin is the most competitive guy he's ever worked with. It's good for his health and helps work off a lot of the energy he has.

One thing I liked to kid about, when the twins were at their most destructive and kicking holes in the walls, was how much they caused me to learn about home repair. I had a friend come down and teach me how to patch walls. I got pretty darn good at fixing drywall. I also felt like an apprentice plumber. The boys continually threw things down the toilets. I had to fish out crazy things all the time. Toys, clothes— you name it. All the time. One year near Christmas, Tickle Me Elmo went to a watery grave. We had to get the septic tank pumped, and the worker came in livid because there were so many things in there. He really lectured me about it. The only comeback I had for him was, "Buddy, if you only had any idea how much else could have been down there."

At twenty-three, Austin and Christian still write letters to Santa and get excited to go to the mall and get in line to tell Santa what they want. Since there are a lot of little kids there, of course, the twins get some curious looks. Ana whispers to parents in line that the twins are still firm believers. The last picture we got of the kids with Santa, Isabella and Christian were smiling at the camera, but Austin didn't care a bit about the picture. He was up close to Santa's ear, reading off his wish list, making sure Santa knew everything he wanted.

Isabella is eleven years younger than Austin and Christian but already has gone through the "Santa Awareness" phase. We had to tell her to be careful around them because they still believe so sincerely, and we're afraid it will just break their hearts. She winked to let us know she could keep the secret.

It's obvious we tell more stories about Austin than Christian because he's so much more outgoing. Christian is harder to engage most of the time, but he's such a wonderful guy. I've got a great relationship with Christian. I'll go up to him and say, "Put up your dukes," with my fists up like we're going to have a mock boxing match. Ana calls it my "messin' with Christian" time. Some of the time, Christian is like, *Go away, Dad.* But I'm always trying to make him smile because it's so rewarding when he does. Ana will come up and tell him I'm just making jokes. "Daddy's just kidding," she'll say, and then he'll laugh.

A lot of times my jokes have to be explained to him—like all the best "dad" humor.

ANA

I understand how people can get confused when they see unfamiliar behavior. But we've never seen our boys be intentionally hurtful or hostile to anybody. No question—they have been destructive at home, but we try to remember, when they get angry, that they tend to be angry with themselves. Dr. Green told us that kids on the spectrum often turn their expressions of pain inward rather than outward. Maybe that makes them more evolved in some ways.

I wish I had known when we were in the middle of the most dramatic phases of the twins' youth that many of the worst behaviors would fade. There are new worries, but we don't feel like we live in a prison of our own making anymore. There's a lot more laughter in the house. For so long we had no idea that was possible, and it was hard to sustain a sense of optimism.

The boys are more flexible now when their schedules get changed. They've learned to be better with the small disappointments of not going somewhere they thought we would, or not getting to do something they had their minds set on. That may seem like a minor thing, but that's a big step that makes every day much easier. As a result, life has really mellowed, so we can enjoy their personalities more.

It's easy to see the goodness in their hearts in the way they're so gentle with Isabella and our three dogs. Austin loves one of them, little Diesel, so much and carries him around. He told me that Diesel is his sidekick. It's the cutest thing. Christian takes joy in being around animals, particularly big animals, like horses. They seem to be so like Christian—big and very, very gentle. I think that being able to connect with animals shows a kind of emotional growth.

For a while we had the twins involved in *hippotherapy*, being around horses. They learned to ride and how to saddle and tack up horses. The tame and docile ones, at least. The boys were calmer after doing it.

Christian has developed the focus to watch a television show other than Disney. He usually doesn't have the patience for shows, or for sitting with us that long, either. But the one he's most keen on is a documentary program about a zoo. It started with a segment about giraffes. At first we were in shock because Christian had never watched an entire show with us. Something about giraffes entirely fascinates him. At other times, when a lion roars, Christian roars back. Now we're trying to think of ways that animal documentaries could be used as some kind of a gateway to effective therapy for him.

Both of the twins have such good hearts and very innocent minds. I want to try to keep it like that. They're in their twenties, but they're still very innocent. I keep an eye on the kinds of things they see on the computer and in movies, and Curt and I always watch our language. They don't seem to have much interest in some of the things that can lure teens or young people into trouble. And that feels like a blessing.

Christian's nature is to be subtle and quiet, but that doesn't mean unexpressive. He'll say things under his breath, so you have to listen closely. When they were getting close to graduation from high school, Christian muttered, "Goodbye, school; goodbye, kids . . . no more Cruellas" (his joking name for some of the ladies who worked with him). While Austin was sad to the point of tears that school would be ending, Christian was delighted to be done with it. Austin loved the social aspects of school; Christian would much rather be on his own.

Christian has grown more comfortable with himself and seems at ease with the roles the twins have carved out for themselves. Austin has always been bigger and stronger and more assertive, always the senior partner, and almost always at a higher stage of development.

I don't think Christian ever saw much benefit in challenging Austin's place in their established pecking order. We thought that this wasn't entirely fair to Christian, so we've tried to balance things out whenever we can, getting Christian some preferential treatment, or at least getting them separated at times so Christian can have more breathing space. But when they're together, they fall into their customary roles, and it usually works well enough that there isn't conflict. One of the twins' chores around the house is to clear the table after dinner. Austin cleans up by eating the last bits of chicken off every bone on the plates, and then Christian cleans up after him, carefully placing the discarded bones in the garbage. That pretty much captures their relationship.

Austin's and Christian's opposite tastes are so obvious in their reaction to one of our nightly rituals. After prayers, Austin always wants me to sing his favorite lullaby: "When You Wish Upon a Star." I'll admit that I'm no Jiminy Cricket when it comes to singing that song, but Austin loves it, and it soothes him. Maybe he likes the predictability of it, night after night. It's something peaceful and optimistic he can count on before bed.

But while Austin loves the song, Christian gets upset. I barely get started with "When You Wish Upon a Star" and Christian starts covering his ears. He despises my singing. In fact, I learned that my singing is a guaranteed way to get Christian to break a cycle of distracting behaviors. When I need to get some work done or to have quiet for a few minutes, I start singing "Let It Go" from the movie *Frozen*. Christian hates my singing so much he drops whatever he's doing and leaves the room.

Everybody's a critic!

CHAPTER 20

TESTED BY FIRE

ANA

The few people who know even a small part of our story have asked how we've kept it all together. Our family, our marriage, our sanity. When we tell them about the things that have given us strength, some say that ours isn't an autism story—it's a love story. I like hearing that because that's exactly what we think it is, too. Although, when you're both in the middle of unspeakably gross cleanup jobs, or constant repairs, it's hard to look at each other and think, *Wow, isn't this the perfect romance?*

We've seen different numbers from various studies, so it's hard to statistically quantify how the pressures of raising special needs children affect marriages. At least anecdotally, it seems accepted that the stresses add to a high incidence of marital troubles. We understand how hard it is for anybody to make a marriage work, but it's especially difficult with such added burdens.

We hit our own lows many, many times, and we know the kind of things that can go through a mind in the dark times. Usually, Curt would find some way to defuse it with a funny story or a bit of gallows humor. ("You know, if I leave you, you'll have the kids all by yourself." *Oh, no, don't go!*)

We both think that having a solid foundation based on our love for each other and our strong faith helped us weather the hard times. We made a promise to one another, and to God, and we were going to stick it out through sickness and health. That meant there was no giving up. These were lessons we both took from our parents. That's what marriage has been to us.

I've heard it said that God laughs at the plans of man. When we got married, it was a fairy tale come to life. It really did seem perfect. And I foolishly expected the rest of our lives would follow accordingly. Now I understand that phrase about the fallibility of the plans of man.

From the start, from the minute the twins were diagnosed, every time I'd dive into the promise of a new treatment, I'd get excited over the possibilities. *This is it! This makes sense. This will be the cure.* And when little came of that exciting new development, it felt like just another failure. Those things add up, and after a while, it seemed like we were fighting against a sense of futility as much as autism.

Curt has had unbelievable patience. Unbelievable! I tell people to forget about his football honors, he deserves to be in a Hall of Fame of Husbands. Anytime I was dealing with the boys on my own and having a hard time, I would call the dealership. Curt would jump in the car and come home. Anytime I was tired and needed to go to bed, even if it was seven in the evening, he would take over. I might sleep until ten in the morning because I was exhausted, and he'd have things under control. He's always had my back. Always.

He always responded respectfully to my lashing out or manic moments. When I was out of control, he might tell me I had gone too far and that he disagreed with me. But there was never disrespect. That, too, was at the core of it for us. Sometimes I'd get angry and cross, and we'd both be frustrated. But when all those things exist in the context of respect, they're not as abrasive.

We never really talked to people about our relationship until now, thinking those things are better left behind our closed doors. But now we're not reluctant to say that our relationship has been tested by fire. Very literally.

Now we start the days by praying together. We pray for each other and for the kids, and give thanks for all the wonderful things in our lives. We try to remember to take joy in the little things and be thankful for them. We have a home, we have wonderful children. So, let's look at that side of things.

I know how rare Curt is. Sometimes all I really needed was his hug, and to hear him tell me we were going to be okay. For me, there was healing power in those things.

That's who he's always been, even back when he guarded his emotions pretty tightly. That's how he's always taken care of me, how he's always taken care of his family, and how humble he is. He makes me laugh, and he's always the fun parent for the kids. And now he just has so much peace about him that he's able to open up and talk about the life we've led.

There is truly no one like him. This man has been my rock all the way, along with my faith—our shared faith. No, our lives didn't stay a fairy tale, but Curt always has been my prince.

CURT

Maybe we were fooling ourselves at times. We never accepted that autism could defeat us. We decided we would never lie down and quit.

When you've got a tiger by the tail, you don't know where it's going—you just have to hang on, have to try to get from day to day. The best way for us to do it was to be there for each other and lean on our faith.

There were seven or eight years after the diagnosis that were very painful for both of us, and I think for a long time we both tried to put up a front. But on the inside, we were both sad and disappointed. When one of us was down, the other had to pick up the slack. If not, we'd both just be wading in self-pity. You can live in that self-pity, or you can just face the fact that there's no way out except to keep fighting to make progress, to make life better in whatever ways you can.

Ana would get angry when she'd work so hard on arranging a treatment for the boys, get her hopes up so high, and then watch that treatment not work. She had to express her frustration. She had to get that rage out. We were living in a fortress. Who else was she going to unload on? She could be short and have a temper, and she could use sarcasm like a dagger.

It was hurtful, sure. But I just felt that getting angry back at her wasn't the right thing to do. I tried to put myself in her shoes. I saw how hectic her days were. I knew how much her heart was hurting. She had been through so much—even before the twins were born. We both had been through so much.

I'm human; I got upset. I got angry, too. I thought that most of the time it was better for me not to express it. I was afraid I might just really lose it. I learned in sports that you can't ever start pointing fingers rather than being accountable for yourself. When you start blaming others for your problems, things start unraveling.

I think it helped that we never looked too far ahead, not even two or three weeks down the road. We had to take life in smaller pieces, just make it to the next day, the next hour. Every night we would regroup, hoping and praying that somehow we could get this situation—this beast—under control.

Ana held herself to such a high standard as a mother, and I think that made her too hard on herself. She worried about what she had done wrong and blamed herself. I had to remind her, *You're not a bad parent because you have children with disabilities. It was not your fault . . . it was not my fault. It just was what it was.* Autism doesn't discriminate. We're Christians, and our faith was tested many, many, many times. We learned that we had to talk about our life honestly. We made the choice to do what we could to keep positive and keep our faith. That's what we've been able to do.

I looked back further, too, to my family, and how strong they were during my childhood. My parents saw poverty and back-breaking labors, and the kind of family strife that led them to adopt me and raise me as their son. None of that could have been easy. But they made it through together. They had happy lives. My parents set the standard and gave me that blueprint to follow, and I wasn't going to expect less of myself.

Ana tells me I'm her rock, but I don't consider myself a rock. I'm just a husband who loves his wife. Now even more than ever.

Austin and Christian at their high school graduation, 2015.

CHAPTER 21

AUSTIN AND CHRISTIAN AS YOUNG MEN

2015–2017

ANA

Austin loved high school, but Christian went through a period of several years when he didn't want to go to school at all. Austin liked being around other people. Christian didn't. He's always been more introverted, but I also think a part of it is he simply wasn't healthy. Many times I had to keep Christian home because of the PANDAS (Pediatric Autoimmune Neuropsychiatric Disorders Associated with Streptococcal

Infections) condition that causes him to be affected by a strep bacteria in his body. That heightens his obsessive-compulsive behavior.

It's gotten easier over time as the twins' behavior has become more related to OCD than the self-stimming or self-injury. As Dr. Green looked at the boys' markers entering adulthood, he saw them with nearly enough language to communicate their basic needs. But their biggest hurdle, he said, was the "obsessive loop they've been stuck in for a long, long time." He related it to a seizure activity in which a part of the brain goes in loops. We can jump in and break the cycle by getting them to focus on something else for a while, but it often just starts up again.

When they were old enough to start getting on iPads and DVD players, that stimulus would keep their attention and calm them, narrowing their field of focus. Rather than getting into their self-stimulation patterns, the boys would be distracted by the videos. We've also worked on relaxation techniques and deep breathing, trying to calm them down through those methods. When they're at the point of a meltdown, we try to deflect them, push them in some other direction. Sometimes pressure on their bodies helps, and there are some sensory stimulations, like holding them or rubbing them, that eases their anxiety.

Since their communication has improved, we've found it helps to actually supply them with the words to identify the feelings they're having. It came together like this: Austin had done something and he was mad at himself, and he was biting his arm really hard. I said, "Austin, you're frustrated," and he looked at me, and said, "I'm frustrated." I said, "Yes, you are, you don't need to bite your arm. You're just frustrated." He understood, said it again, and he calmed down. It was like the steam valve on a pressure cooker; it kept him from exploding into a meltdown.

In Christian's last years in school, his OCD intensified and would cause him to get stuck in one behavior. I was called to the school once because teachers thought he was having a seizure. He was so frozen that they weren't sure he was breathing. It was very sad to see him this way, and also very scary because it was a new behavior, one we had no idea how to cope with. We had to keep him home for a few days because that behavior was so intense. When the OCD reaches critical levels, he's not able to function. He literally would take two steps forward, two steps back, and sometimes he would yell for help because he couldn't stop himself. At times he would freeze in place for minutes.

As the compulsiveness increased, Christian lost language skills and regressed in other ways. He was further ahead at seventeen than at twenty. That led to his repeatedly making a grinding noise and biting one of his fingers to the point that a callus developed. Even today, when he gets up to use the bathroom, Christian will repeatedly turn the light switch on and off. Many, many times.

Austin, meanwhile, has been diagnosed with Lyme disease; we have no idea how he contracted it.

Even after graduation, they still needed help with their hygiene. Austin could start the job of shaving, but missed patches that I had to touch up. I had to do it entirely for Christian.

A therapist who worked with them through the years as they matured, and who has experience with children across the spectrum, said she would classify Austin and Christian "on the lower end" of the spectrum as they finished up with school.

In June 2015, Austin and Christian got their caps and gowns and received their diplomas for having made it through the special education program at Camas High. They were twenty. The last two years in school, they were part of a program of transitional education that focused on life skills.

At that time, their instructors and therapists at school gave them individualized evaluations, which outlined their strengths and future possibilities. Curt and I loved seeing the itemized expectations for the boys since we'd spent so much time hearing about all the things we'd never see them do. This was a chance to learn about their strengths from people who weren't biased like we were.

Austin's evaluation touted his leadership ability, determination, and strength. Future possibilities included outdoor work, materials handling, warehouse work, gardening, and typing information onto computers. His requirements for success included structure and consistency.

Christian's report cited his friendly, sweet nature, and his tolerance. He sorted bolts and screws while in the program, and the instructors cited his ability to stack/bag items and work with animals. He does best with structure and clear expectations.

To hear that there were certain situations in which they could focus and finish a task and use tools was so heartening. Their graduation from high school was not a matter of scholastic achievement, but of their reaching the age when they are no longer a part of the special education system.

They worked for a time with Habitat for Humanity, and Christian was able to use power tools and take lamps apart. The report from the organization was that they were hardworking and proud of themselves. They had a script of what they were supposed to be doing, and if they went off script or got distracted, the manager only had to tap that script, and they would understand they had to focus on their work again.

The twins continued to work with therapists and aides in situations available to special needs employees. The goal was to phase out the aid as much as possible so they could become more independent.

Christian also worked for a while at a produce store breaking down boxes and following instructions on where to carry and place them. He enjoyed the work, even though it was only for an hour at a time. Austin is particularly tech savvy, so we always thought he might have some opportunities in that area.

At twenty, they were evaluated as having the learning ability of boys who are five or six, or perhaps, in terms of school, Christian was like a first grader and Austin a second grader.

While they are more consistent in their manners and behavior, they can still surprise us with unexpected behavior. Especially Austin. I bought some new earbud headphones for Christian that he could wear while working to help cancel out distracting noise. I found the empty packaging on the floor and asked Christian how his new headphones were working out. He said he didn't have them.

"What happened?" I assumed he lost them.

"Austin ate them," he said.

CURT

There were some practical things we hadn't anticipated when Austin and Christian turned eighteen and, from a legal standpoint, became adults. We had to go before a judge to petition for total guardianship. Otherwise, we'd never be able to get disclosure from the boys' doctors, and other kinds of health and safety communications could get tangled in legal obstacles. We were getting all kinds of stuff, like the US Army wanting to talk to them about enlistment, or banks trying to get them to sign up for credit cards all the time.

We had begun getting calls from the pharmacy asking to speak with Christian Warner about his medication. We'd say, "You can't really talk to him, we're his parents." Once he was eighteen, they'd say they had to speak to Christian himself. We'd try to explain, and they would tell us that by law they could only speak to Christian. We'd say, "Okay, we'll get him to the phone, you can ask him about his prescriptions, and we'll see how that goes." By petitioning for their legal guardianship, we now can handle those situations.

There are more important long-term legal implications of our guardianship, and as the twins transitioned into adulthood, the process helped reinforce in our minds how crucial it was to have their future living and care circumstances set and in place.

CHAPTER 22

WARNERS AT WORK

ANA

At twenty-three, the twins are employed on a part-time basis, and they enjoy work a great deal. Actually, Austin likes to go to work to make money . . . Christian likes to go to work to get away from Austin.

They work five days a week, in two-hour shifts, for SEH America in Vancouver, Washington. The company is a silicon-wafer semiconductor manufacturer that employs more than twenty people with intellectual disabilities. It's wonderful that this company is committed to helping train and employ workers and focus on people's abilities, not their disabilities. SEH has specialists come in and set up adaptations to jobs that give people like Austin and Christian a chance to be successful.

It gives them more than a chance; it gives them hope.

Austin is a production assistant. He scrapes labels off shipping boxes, handles some shipping information, and then has some cleanup duties. He loves to be around people and talk to them—a little too much at times. When it's time to work, he has to be reminded to focus on the job, so they have him mostly working by himself. But he's very productive, and he's very good at it. He's a hard worker and he's strong. Though he continues to adapt to the job in some ways, his bosses really like him and they want to keep him. They've been very willing to work with us on any issues that have come up.

Mostly Austin likes getting a paycheck. He understands the process: he goes to work, he gets paid, and then he can buy things he wants. He's always looking to get things on eBay or Amazon. It's still mostly Disney stuff. His room is full of books of Disney art. He's also interested in old movie projectors and large-format films.

Christian works in the uniform distribution center. He knows how to work the computer; he puts the numbers in and scans the uniforms. He's doing great and likes his job. He's had a few hiccups as well, but they're working with us on making everything go smoother.

Christian is a little bit more comfortable socially when he's there, and he's learning to like working with people more. But he doesn't have the interest in money that Austin does. He doesn't have much desire to buy anything.

They both look forward to going to work and take pride in it. We couldn't be more grateful for the opportunities they're getting. We always worried whether there would be employment suited to them. Companies like SEH are proving there are places for workers like Austin and Christian.

Jonathan has a new job, too. After finishing up his broadcast journalism degree at Penn State, he became the cohost and executive producer of a sports radio talk show in Portland (Rip City/iHeart Radio, 620). He loves it, staying around sports and talking about them all day.

I am also taking some of the things I learned through our experience with autism and putting them to use. I spent a lot of time researching healthy eating and how nutrition affects your life. Aside from researching for the boys, I also got a firsthand feel for how better nutrition can help you. When I was diagnosed with chronic fatigue, I improved my diet, and I could see how much better it made me feel. I'm now halfway through my classes with the Institute for Integrative Nutrition, studying to be a health coach.

CURT

In 2010, I'd been in the car business since I got out of the NFL, and I felt it was time for a change. Not that I didn't like it, it was just time to move on for a combination of reasons. Plus, I loved the idea of changing and growing and finding new professional opportunities. I'm always open to new challenges. So I got my insurance license and got into a Farmers Insurance agency in Portland.

Insurance is an industry that is very competitive. I like the fact that you can assist and advise people with their policies and help them make smart decisions about protecting themselves. You're more of a consultant than anything, looking at clients' coverages and helping them get what they need. I can tell them from personal experience how important insurance is, having experienced a house fire myself.

It's a business that lets me deal with people every day. There's a puzzle-solving quality to it, too, matching their coverages to their needs. I enjoy getting to know the clients and hearing their stories. I'm not sure, especially in Portland, how many old Seahawks fans I run into. But if they want to buy insurance when they talk about football, that's fine with me.

Most of the time, now, when people connect my name to the NFL, they're thinking about the Kurt Warner who was the quarterback for the Rams and the Cardinals. He came along quite a bit later. Sometimes I'll get requests for autographed pictures from people trying to reach *Kurt Warner*. I should start sending them my pictures—and maybe try to sell them some insurance, too.

CHAPTER 23

RECOVERY AND CONTROVERSY

ANA

We try to be very cautious about the terms we use regarding ASD. So many heated discussions arise from the different perspectives on the disorder, and terminology is often a trigger for debate. Autism is an emotional topic, and we like to be sensitive to those whose lives are touched by it. For instance, some prefer the term *child with autism* rather than *autistic child*, believing that the child may have the disorder, but is not specifically defined by it, as it seems when the word is used as a modifier.

The discussions of recovery, cure, and improvements prompt debates, too, and the term *normal* carries the implication that those with ASD are something less than normal. Some, then, prefer the term *neurotypical.* Curt and I want to be respectful of all these concerns, and we try to avoid labels and assumptions.

With the twins hitting adulthood, we know they still are heavily impacted by autism. We prayed for a cure, although the word *recovered* is a term some prefer. They are healthier and their lives seem less painful, but our boys are not cured or recovered.

They are much better behaved. They're not as destructive anymore, and that's made a huge difference in our lives. I could never get used to the idea that something was constantly getting broken in our house. It wasn't a concern for the walls or furniture but for the kids. We'd learned that when something was breaking, it could mean somebody was getting hurt.

We were always on guard, but now our reflexes don't have to be on hair triggers as much. To be out of that phase is liberating. There isn't nearly as much worry about somebody being injured.

Their temperaments are more stable, and their ability to focus has increased. Those should be positive developments as they continue in the workforce.

Dr. Green told us that there have been studies around the country of children who have had very significant recoveries, but the medical community hasn't been able to really decide why it happens. Most of those kids who become more functional, he said, generally have some residual symptoms like anxiety or ADHD-type issues. In some cases, they need time to adapt and integrate after having been on the sidelines, socially, for a long time.

But significant improvement has happened in some cases of ASD.

We have taken a lot of hope from the experience of our friends Bill and Jo Krueger and their daughter, Chanel. Bill pitched in the major leagues for thirteen seasons, and his career with the Seattle Mariners overlapped Curt's with the Seahawks. We were neighbors in Redmond, Washington, when the kids were little.

Their daughter was diagnosed with ASD when she was very young, and she regressed to being almost fully nonverbal. She wouldn't speak, wouldn't sleep, and wouldn't let her parents touch her. But with intense therapy, Chanel regained her ability to communicate and was able to mainstream through high school and college. At the time we were writing this book, Chanel was in her third year of the Seattle University School of Law. The Kruegers felt the breakthrough came when they were able to get Chanel to start communicating again. Jo Krueger saw the same kinds of insensitive reactions to her daughter in public that we also experienced. Jo tried to educate people rather than get upset. Whenever somebody might be rude, Jo would stop and ask, "How can I help you understand this?" I was inspired by her approach and the wonderful work they did with their daughter. Chanel is quite a success story, and proof that, in some cases, significant changes can occur.

Opinions on autism and its effects span a broad spectrum, too. And they tend to be highly charged emotionally. How could they not? It involves caring parents trying to decide what's best for their children. In my online studies and scouring for news of treatments and developments, I've seen a common debate over a hypothetical question: Would you change your child with autism if you could?

We love our boys. We love them just the way they are. But they've had so much pain. So we would change that, of course. Even though their world seems to be an easier place now, they're still dealing with significant health troubles and certain limitations.

Some parents with children on the spectrum say there's nothing to cure. It's just how their children are, and they should be cherished that way. It's just a different normal for them. I think the children of those parents must be at least fairly high functioning. Good for them. I applaud their perspective.

At one point, Christian told a little story about love: "Grow up . . . love . . . get married." That meant to us that Christian sees that path as a typical human process. We would give anything to see that be something our twins could experience, to be independent and self-sufficient. We think it will be unlikely for them to drive a car, go to college, to be on their own. One day, Austin was saying, "No girlfriend . . . just Austin and Christian." He knew that when Jonathan graduated, he had a girlfriend. The twins have not shown any interest in that kind of relationship, but it's obvious that they notice the difference. That's my perspective—and I respect the view of others—but to me, it's heartbreaking.

Dr. Green told us that often when kids have some cognitive improvement, they experience more hurt about being different. They want to know why. They start to notice and think about how they are different from others, and they realize they're not experiencing the same things in life. That can be tough on them.

We cherish our twins, and we hurt for them when they hurt. We would do anything for them to get relief from physical and emotional suffering.

I'll never forget the day when Austin called me "Mom," and then later told me he loved me. I guess parents typically hear that "mom" verbalization early. When children start to speak, their first words are usually *mama* or *dada*. And that's, what, usually around one? And then pretty soon they'll usually say "luv you" or something that sounds like it in response to an "I love you" from their parents. It took so long for us to hear even a few words from either of the twins. Austin was almost six years old when he said, "Mama." (And Christian was much older.) We were afraid they'd never be able to understand or communicate that basic concept. And when I heard Austin say it the first time? Oh, I must have scared him by giving him so many kisses and crying so hard.

Communication with your children is something parents might take for granted. It was 2004 before Christian said his first unprompted sentence. He was nine.

The rate of autism is growing. According to the Centers for Disease Control and Prevention, one in sixty-eight children in America has ASD. There's a lot of passion in the debate over the impact of vaccinations on the rate of autism. Some believe that vaccines contribute to autism, and others feel there are a number of contributing factors and that vaccines have nothing to do with it. If debates lead people to understand and investigate medical possibilities, that's great. Discussions can't be bad if they help find answers.

Curt and I are not against vaccinations, but based on our experience, we have concerns about the timing and frequency with which they're scheduled. Between the time when Jonathan received his vaccinations and the time when the twins were getting vaccinated, the number of shots had increased considerably, and the period over which they received vaccinations had been compressed a great deal. We also wonder how vaccinations may affect children who might be sick when they get them. Christian, for instance, was always on antibiotics for infections when he was getting vaccinated.

Whether these things played a role in their autism, there's no way to know, and we'd rather focus on finding a cure rather than pinning blame. Our boys have seen Dr. Green for a number of years, and we trust him wholeheartedly. He has treated more than three thousand patients with ASD around the world. When he's asked what causes autism, he's very straightforward in his response: "I don't know."

In 2013, Curt and I were asked to speak at the National Autism Conference at Penn State. We spoke to the crowd about never giving up on our boys or losing our hope that they'll get healthier over time. We found ourselves sharing this passion with those other parents of ASD kids—regardless of their position on the many-faceted debates. We all hoped that someday our concerns will help in finding a cure.

Raising awareness is of global value, because autism isn't specific to American children, of course. A 2011 report by the Yale Child Study Center found that the rate of autism was one in thirty-eight children in South Korea; and Japan, the United Kingdom, Sweden, and Denmark also have rates higher than the United States.

It's evident that there's a shortage of attention being paid around the world. Dr. Green told us he was visited by a doctor from China who has a child with autism. She was about to become the first doctor in China to specialize in treating the disorder. It's unimaginable—a massive country like China having *one* doctor focused on autism.

CURT

I trust the medical profession and the innovations doctors are capable of making. When I tore my knee up my second season in the NFL, Dr. Scranton took a ligament from my hamstring to rebuild my ACL. At the time, it was a pioneering surgery, and I know it allowed me to extend my career. Now, knee injuries are often fixed with a minimally invasive scope, and players are back on the field within a very short time—sometimes weeks. Doctors have figured out a way to fix knees better and faster.

I would love to see that kind of progress made toward the treatment of autism and ultimately discovering a cure for it. Fixing a complex neurological disorder isn't like repairing a knee, obviously. It's not a direct comparison, but it gives me reason to hope that time and research can solve the mysteries of ASD.

I don't really enjoy the hypothetical debates surrounding autism, so when somebody asks me if I would change the twins if I could, I just immediately think, *Of course I would.* I don't have to take much time to explain why, either. No parent wants to see their child suffering. So many times we've seen them hurt themselves. We've seen them unhealthy. We've seen them in pain. We've seen them terribly unhappy. I don't think anybody can see their kids banging their heads on the floor and think it's something that doesn't desperately need to be cured.

People shape their opinions based on their own experiences, and only they can say how they feel inside about such things. We respect that. We're not interested in making judgments. Everybody has their own stories and can agree or disagree. We can only relate to what we've seen and experienced.

I would love it if nobody ever had to go through that. Not kids. Not parents. Nobody.

The Warner family.

CHAPTER 24

THE NEXT CHAPTER

2017

ANA

A 2013 study by the *Journal of the American Academy of Child & Adolescent Psychiatry* cited the unemployment/underemployment rate of people on the spectrum as 90 percent—higher than any other disability group. That's a huge concern considering the growing number of those being diagnosed with ASD.

There is a name for the surge of newly matured adults with ASD: the Autism Tsunami. Dr. Reid deals with this all the time and says the numbers are nearing a crisis stage, with an estimated half a million persons with autism aging out of the system of social aid in the next ten years. She said the likelihood is that the numbers will continue to increase.

Dr. Reid knew of only one person hired to do job training for young adults with autism in the state of Oregon. That woman's task was to teach personal finances, shopping, housekeeping, bill paying, and other practical day-to-day matters. It's a wonderful program, but obviously understaffed.

We don't know where our twins' abilities will take them or whether their strengths can be translated into self-supporting work over the long term. We had no way to predict as they aged whether there would be development or regression, or if better therapies would become available. The uncertainty made planning for the future difficult. But here we are, with adult sons who need care, financial support, and structured supervision.

A couple hours east of Seattle, in Ellensburg, is the Trellis Center, a nonprofit ranch and farm specializing in the support and development of adults with disabilities. Curt and I are building a home at the Sunridge Ranch, there, for the twins. It will be their asset, and, as such, provide long-term security. There are live-in aides and counselors to teach daily living skills, as well as vocational and social skills. The boys will work with crops and care for animals on the ranch. Living there will provide them with employment and schooling and care for the rest of their lives.

Austin, particularly, is looking forward to moving. He tells anyone who will listen that he's going to move to Ellensburg and live with his friends. I asked if we can come and visit, and Austin said, "Yes, stay my house." He understands it will be their place.

I've been taking care of the twins 24-7 all their lives. It's going to be a good thing for them to have a safe and secure long-term residence, but I will miss them. I'm looking forward to spending more time with Isabella, though, who has mixed feelings about the boys moving out. They've been such a huge part of her life.

It's going to be different, it's going to be hard, but the twins are excited about it. The only problem they seem to have with the decision is that we can't tell them exactly when they'll move in yet. They're desperate to know when they'll get started.

CURT

There was the faint hope that the twins would recover somewhat as they aged, that they'd become more high functioning and somewhat self-sufficient as they got older. They've improved, but it's not like they could manage on their own. They will always need to have aid if there is no further recovery.

Somebody has to make sure the boys are not going to be mistreated or abused, that they're happy and safe, and the plan to move them to the ranch at the Trellis Center achieves this.

This won't stop us from worrying, but we'll feel a lot better about their long-term living situation. They would own the house, so it couldn't be taken away from them, and we all can still be involved and visit and be in touch all the time. I feel at ease knowing that if something happened to Ana and me, the twins would be settled, and Jonathan and Isabella wouldn't be left facing a huge financial burden.

I like to think that Austin and Christian's relationship with each other will help them. They currently don't interact much, but they have an understanding that the other one should be there, and we'd never want to see them get separated.

We're hoping that in a place of their own, with supervision and structure and daily therapies and appropriate work, they will flourish. It might be better for them in some ways, because they'll have access to more activities and there will be people around all the time who are trained to care for people with ASD. Living at this facility will help them be more productive, and maybe they will keep making progress with their health and development. That's my hope.

CHAPTER 25

YOU ARE NOT ALONE

ANA

I hope the rising awareness of autism will help reduce the level of intolerance that we saw back when our twins were young. So often people would just assume our kids were misbehaving and throwing temper tantrums. People would come up to us and tell us we needed to discipline our kids more. Sometimes I wished we had T-shirts for the kids that said, "I have autism, don't judge me."

So many times when I would take the boys to Dr. Green's office for appointments, I would look at the pictures of his patients that he keeps tacked up on his walls. It looks like a wall of fame to me. I think those kids are real heroes, they're so tough.

Autism is so frequently a subject on the news now, and even television shows feature characters with autism. There's an awareness in the culture that wasn't there before, and that has to be good for funding research and public understanding. I don't imagine people get as many cold and judgmental looks now when their child has a meltdown or begins stimming in public.

After twenty years, we've got a better sense of peace about our lives. Maybe it comes with age, or all the things we've learned through accumulated experience. We still worry, but we can talk about it more openly now, and we're more realistic about our expectations.

I still ask myself a lot of the same questions. *Could I have done something differently? Did I do the best I could?* I think most mothers worry about those things, but I've reached a point where I can stop second-guessing myself. I know that even when things went wrong along the way, I had the best intentions for my children.

I once read that if the wind doesn't change, you have to reset your sails to get to where you need to be. That sums up our story. We learned to redefine our idea of healing. For the boys, it's been in small increments, some steps gained and some lost. But as a family, we've found contentment even though our circumstances haven't changed much. It was a healing in our hearts that we needed desperately.

The fire that burned down our house forced us all to reshape our attitudes. Especially me. And maybe I was the one who needed it the most. We lost almost everything, but we learned that it was just stuff. That's all it was—stuff. Stuff isn't what makes you happy; your family is what makes you happy. It took the fire for me to be reminded of that.

By surrendering my fixation on control, I became more content. My life is still chaotic. But I have a feeling of peace about it. Our kids are safe. Our kids are such good people, with good hearts—as are so many of the other ASD kids we've met.

Curt says he doesn't see much point in looking back. To him, it's best to just move forward. But I do look back, and I'm amazed. There was something that made me feel so strongly about coming to America.

Something that led me to Curt from half a world away, and that something caused us to build this family.

I like the Maya Angelou quote, "When you learn, teach. When you get, give."

We have our love, we have our faith, and we were blessed with a loving family. *Hope*, *faith*, and *love*—these are three words Curt and I say to each other all the time. We wanted to share that learning and give it to others.

We had no idea what we were doing when we were introduced to autism. We ended up finding our way. It wasn't always pretty—except when it was perfect. One day, in particular, I'll never forget.

We had been sent to Colorado for a new treatment involving light and sound therapy that was supposed to be good for kids with autism.

The flight was uneventful, but when we landed at the Denver airport, Christian had a major meltdown, dropping to the floor and violently banging his head. Christian was screaming, pulling his ears, flapping his hands, making strange sounds . . . out of control. People were walking by and looking at us, and you know they're thinking: *What's wrong with these people?* But when the kids have a meltdown, all you can do is ride out the storm. I tried to tend to Austin while Curt tried to calm Christian. People gathered around, and I heard someone ask, "What are you doing to this kid, abusing him?"

Curt did the only thing he could think of: in the middle of a concourse in the busy Denver airport with people gathering around us, he got down on the floor beside his distraught son, quietly trying to reassure him that he was there for him and things would be all right. Here was this well-known former All-NFL football player down on the floor in the middle of a crowded airport concourse, hugging his son, holding his head in his hands to protect him, and talking softly to comfort him.

I would bet that somewhere people who were there that day still talk about this wonderful, sensitive man attending to his son. How could you not love a man who acts with such dignity, grace, and selflessness?

I thought it was so inspiring. I'm brought to tears whenever I think about that moment.

CURT

I never wanted to revisit all this. To remember what those kids went through year after year was to scratch at a lot of old wounds. Looking back and dwelling on everything ran counter to the ways I had learned to cope with the hardships. It always helped me to look forward to short spans of time, from the immediate moment to the next day. It felt easier to handle things in smaller pieces. Focusing on the big picture, that big unknown future, could stop you in your tracks. So, I would deal with whatever was going on that day the best I could, and then find little boxes in my mind where I would put those things away. I'd tuck them in there, and then I could move on. Telling our story meant I'd have to get back into all those little boxes.

There were almost twenty years of symptoms and treatments and times that were painful for everyone in the family. We had a lot going on, and to tell the truth, it made me want to cry about half the time.

Pastor Ken Hutcherson told us some time ago that he thought our story might help other people. That we should write a book about it. Ana laughed . . . as if we had time for that. And I could never see myself being willing to go back over everything that happened—especially to tell complete strangers.

The first time I even considered that there might be positives worth sharing was after we spoke at the National Autism Conference in 2013. That was the first time we told our story, the first time I could get up in front of people and talk about our experiences without breaking down. We put everything in a PowerPoint presentation with bullet points that went up on a screen, and it wasn't as painful as I thought. Sharing started to feel conversational and personal—like talking to friends.

My emotions got to me at times during the presentation. Ana sensed when it was coming and jumped in and took over until I got squared away and could continue. After that event, many people told us our presentation was meaningful to them. I was very surprised by how strong the response was. Really floored by it, actually. People seemed moved by what we had to say. Some came up and told us they'd been through many of the same things, and it was comforting for them to see how we handled it. Hearing that other people have been through similar things makes your own experiences a little less scary. It was like we were speaking the same language, something that so many other people couldn't really understand.

Now when we speak to groups, our primary message to those in an autistic family is that you're not alone. And we are proof that the experience doesn't have to break you. And once we got started, telling it all has felt therapeutic.

In my case, it made me grow in some very important ways. I think back to when I didn't want to even talk about this to Hutch, somebody I trusted completely. I didn't think talking about these things was appropriate for a man. I feared it would sound like complaining, like I wasn't tough enough to face it.

But now I have no trouble standing up in front of a convention of hundreds of strangers and telling them that I've cried. I've cried so often I couldn't count the times. I used to think that wasn't being a man. I was wrong; that was part of being a human, part of having feelings and loving people who are in pain. And it was part of dealing with the things so many other people have to deal with in life. Life humbles you. And in a lot of ways, that's a good thing. I'm more able to recognize my own emotions and my own shortcomings.

After some of these speaking engagements, I've had people come up and tell me how moved they were by one specific thing I said, above all others. It's when I tell them that I love my wife more now than the day we were married. After all the difficult years, and all the tough times, we're closer than ever. I've seen Ana's strength. I've seen the depth of her love, and I know I'm stronger for having gone through this life with her. She sometimes tells people that I'm her hero. I get a little embarrassed by that. But I can truly come back by saying she's certainly my hero.

It's been a tough, long road, but we got here . . . together.

ACKNOWLEDGMENTS

We subscribe to the idea that it takes a village to raise children. It takes one to write a book, too. We've had a lot of help along the way, and we're eternally grateful to those many who have been so generous with their time and effort.

We would like to thank our Lord and Savior, Jesus Christ, for giving us His strength and grace and mercy and kindness.

To Curt's family: Thanks so much for the lifetime of love and support, particularly sister Joyce and her kids, and brother Robert. Thanks to Pauline Forte for helping us, as well.

To Ana's family: Love and deepest thanks to Mom and Dad—we know how hard it was to see your youngest daughter get on a plane, not knowing if you were going to see her again. You put her dream of living in the United States ahead of your dream that she would raise her family close to you. To sister Maria Carmen, thank you for allowing your daughters Ana Flavia, Fernanda, Bruna, and Barbara to visit and help us for long periods of time. Thank you also for taking care of Mom during her illness and for being there when she passed away. And to brothers Alfredo and Junior, thank you for supporting Ana and being there for Mom and Dad. And to our other nieces and nephews—love to you all!

To the late Dr. Ken Hutcherson, our brother, friend, and pastor— you were so meaningful in our lives! We love you and miss you a lot! Thanks to our dear friend Pat Hutcherson and to Hulia Mae Hutcherson

(Grandma), who gave us endless love and prayers. It was Hutch who told us many years ago that we should consider writing a book about our experiences, since it might help others facing challenges in their lives. To the Hutcherson kids—Faith, Avery, Sherman, and Curtis—we love you and are so glad you're all part of our family.

To our friends the Riveras: Jerry and Donna were particularly comforting and helpful when the twins were young. Jerry, Curt's service manager at the car dealership, sadly passed away in 2004. They were always there for us.

We also would like to mention our Brazilian friends who were part of Ana's life in America: Diva Andrade, Silvia Faria, Nadya Rodriguez, Raul Palacios, Marta Zenger, and Raquel and Greg Prindle. Thank you for all the love and support.

Neighbors Alison and Don Lovell put up with so much from us and have been so generous with their hospitality and unconditional love. Thank you so much. We love you!

Drs. Jennifer Reid and John A. Green III did so much more than just treat Austin and Christian. They were so patient and compassionate with the boys—and us—during so many years of drama and pain and fear.

Helyn Rosemurgy was crucial in getting us started with ABA therapy, helping us in the early stages of understanding autism spectrum disorder, and going with us to IEP meetings. Thank you for your friendship!

Shawn Maepa Horn and Robin Sobotka, thank you for all the hard work of putting a team of therapists together and training them. Along the way, dozens of other therapists invested their time and expertise in the treatment of the twins.

Thanks to those at Trinity Lutheran School in Portland, Oregon, particularly former principal James Riedl and first-grade teacher Nancy Mann, for taking our kids in as part of their ministry. We're eternally grateful for your love, grace, and understanding.

So many neighbors were kind, patient, and understanding, and were truly there for us when we needed them most. Thank you so much to all of them, and also to the brave people in the Camas-Washougal Fire Department and Camas Police Department. For them, the simple "thank you" doesn't feel like enough.

Pastors Karl Payne and Mark Webster at Antioch Bible Church also deserve our deep appreciation. Thanks, too, to Antioch Adoptions for guiding us and for helping us find the blessing of adoption!

Curt's former Seahawks teammate, the late Dave Brown, and his wife, Rhonda, were great mentors to us. And Karen Koehler, one of Ana's best friends in Seattle, was immeasurably comforting and close after we lost our son Ryan.

Jo and Bill Krueger share a bond with us, and their raising of their lovely daughter, Chanel, has been inspiring to us.

Our dear friend Ritchie Coleman, "Uncle Ritchie" to the kids, has always been willing to help repair the damage to our house.

The people at Employers Overload have been wonderful in helping Austin and Christian find work, and, in general, furthering the cause of employment for people with disabilities.

We still feel as if the Seattle Seahawks organization and their fans are part of our family, as well as fans from Penn State, who have been so supportive. Tim Curley played an important role in recruiting Curt to Penn State so many years ago. We continue to appreciate the friendship and support of Tim and his wife, Melinda.

Gary Wright, a long-time executive of the Seahawks, was particularly helpful in getting this book started.

We would like to thank our friend and coauthor Dave Boling. Dave's love and enthusiasm for our story was truly contagious. He spent hours talking to us about it and it felt like good therapy for us. We're eternally grateful for all that he has done to make this dream come true.

We would also like to thank those who have donated to our GoFundMe account (https://www.gofundme.com/curtwarner-s-sons).

Your contributions are greatly appreciated. We initially established this fund to help us with the construction of our twins' home, with the goal of eventually funding more affordable homes for other adults with autism. We wish to thank in advance those who would consider donating to this cause.

If you're interested in speaking to an Information & Referral Specialist, contact The Autism Society's Contact Center at 1-800-3-AUTISM (800-328-8476) or info@autism-society.org. For additional resources visit Autism Source at autismsource.org.

ABOUT THE AUTHORS

Curt Warner is an honors graduate in communication, a two-time All-American at Penn State, 2009 College Football Hall of Fame inductee, and a former All-Pro running back for the Seattle Seahawks and Los Angeles Rams. A three-time Pro Bowler, Warner was inducted into the Seattle Seahawks Ring of Honor in 1994.

Ana Warner has dedicated her life to the care of her family and the study and treatment of autism spectrum disorder. Both she and her husband have served as keynote speakers at the National Autism Conference at Penn State and the Texas Autism Conference in San Antonio. *The Warner Boys* is their first book.

Dave Boling is an award-winning sports columnist and former reporter for the *Tacoma News Tribune*. He is the author of two novels, *Guernica* and *The Lost History of Stars*.